A Year of PRAYER EVENTS for Your Church

BY SANDRA HIGLEY

TERRE HAUTE, INDIANA

PrayerShop Publishing is the publishing arm of Harvest Prayer Ministries and the Church Prayer Leaders Network. Harvest Prayer Ministries exists to make every church a house of prayer.

Its online prayer store, www.prayershop.org, has more than 400 prayer resources available for purchase.

ISBN: 978-0-9793611-7-3

Printed in the United States of America
1 2 3 4 5 6 7 8 9 10 | 2011 2010 2009 2008 2007

Table of Contents

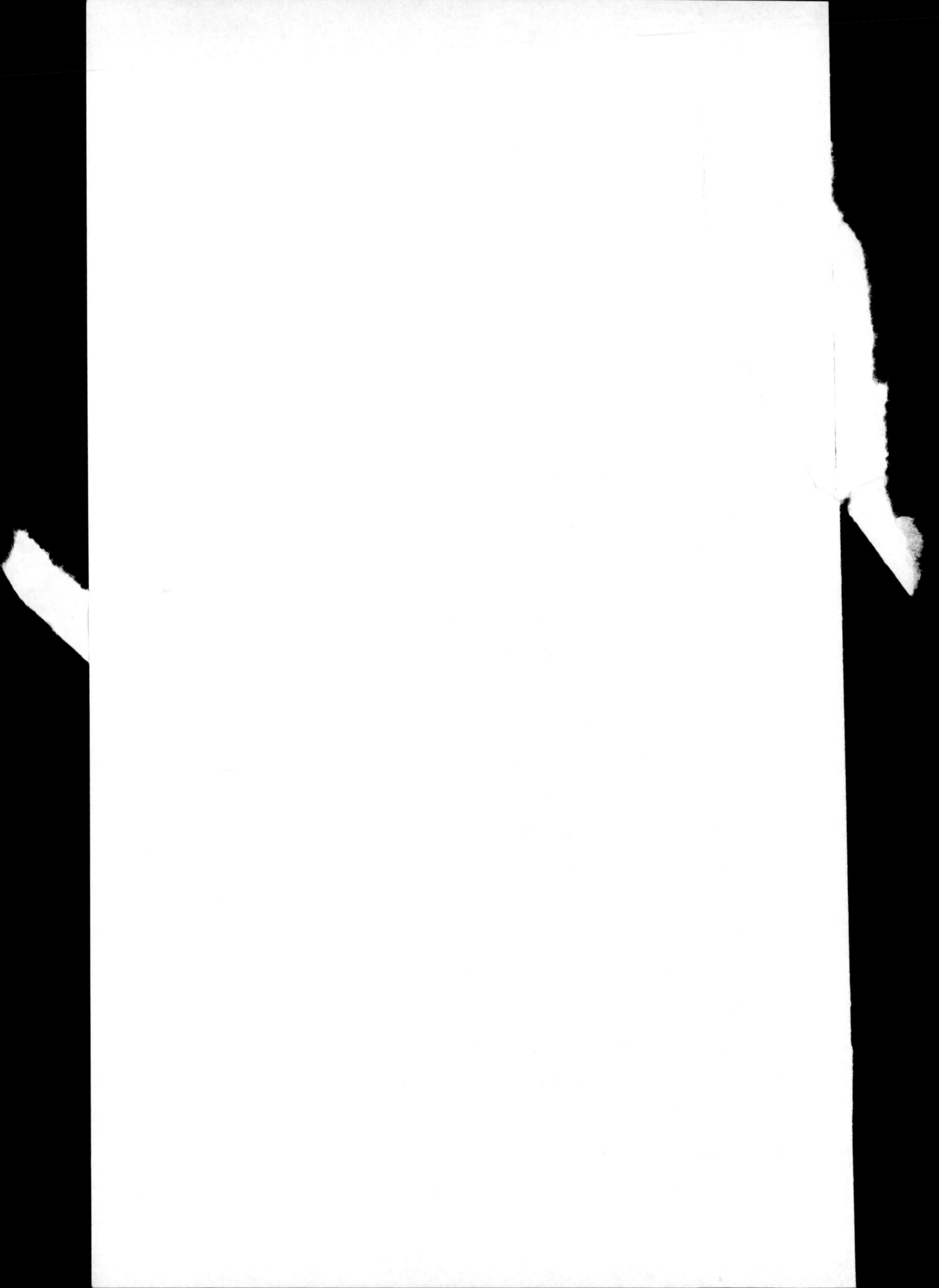

Foreword

I remember my first experience of being a prayer leader in a local church. It was in my early days at *Pray!* magazine. I received lots of ideas through my role at *Pray!* and was anxious to try them out at church.

Unfortunately I was pretty much a flop. Nothing seemed to work. I think it was partly because I was not embarking on a plan—I was just trying to do what worked other places. Another reason was that I was often not prepared enough when I started a new prayer opportunity. I was shooting in the dark. Some things worked well, but a number of things did not. I wish I had had a book like *A Year of Prayer Events for Your Church.*

More and more these days churches are recognizing the importance of developing praying people. They understand that God releases power through a praying church. As a result these churches want effective prayer opportunities to put before their people. They want more than the tired old Wednesday night prayer meeting of the past. They want dynamic events that thoroughly engage those who attend.

In *A Year of Prayer Events for Your Church*, Sandra Higley has provided just that. That's what makes this book so valuable. These pages include everything you need to put on 15 possible prayer events. All the details—schedules, guides, resources—everything a prayer leader would need to pull off the events are included. There are prayer events for kids and adults—both for men and women.

The result is that a church can highlight prayer every month of the year. Why is that important? The more people hear about prayer—through announcements, posters, participation opportunities—the more they will pray. The more they pray, the more they will connect with God, gain the Father's heart and grow spiritually.

I have known Sandra Higley for more than a dozen years—since the very beginnings of the development of *Pray!* magazine. I know she is a woman of prayer. She attends a church that prays. She reflects that experience and passion throughout this book. That's why this book can impact your church in a powerful way.

Jonathan Graf
President
Church Prayer Leaders Network

Introduction

The biggest challenge for any prayer leader—volunteer or paid staff member—is to keep fresh prayer opportunities available to their congregation. Most people in the church body are unfamiliar with prayer outside of the agonizing experiences they've had in the past with dry, mind-numbing Wednesday night prayer meetings. They need to be "coaxed." Any experienced, successful prayer leader will tell you that each prayer event offered to the church is like a fishing net cast into a lake. Every attempt will garner a few more "catches": people who are floundering as they look for purpose. What a delight when they discover the kingdom value and fulfillment of prayer!

Scheduled prayer events are beneficial on many levels. At best, your entire church will catch the vision and earnestly push toward becoming a house of prayer. Even if you don't see immediate outward signs, it will nudge people closer to a personal prayer commitment. Incorporating prayer events into your church calendar shows the importance that church leadership places on prayer. It is a constant reminder that prayer has value and is something to be cultivated personally and corporately. Even though these prayer events are enjoyable, they are more unifying than the typical potluck social. Attendees connect on a deeper level when they come together with a common goal and shared burden. No other planned, church-wide event will benefit the spiritual health and well-being of your church body or fulfill the biblical mandate to "pray without ceasing" as an organized prayer event.

How to Use This Book

This book was prepared in order to get your creative juices flowing when it comes to prayer. Included are ideas for keeping prayer opportunities fresh and frequent. Although monthly prayer events are offered, be sensitive to what works best for your church. It is important to offer opportunities on a regular basis so that your members don't lose interest, but your church might be better suited to an event every other month or even quarterly.

This book was formatted using a September to August calendar year in keeping with the typical church "new year" in the fall. But it is flexible enough to allow you to jump in anywhere in the cycle. The September offering of a "kick-off" seminar is suggested as the launch for your church since it will offer teaching on prayer basics to better equip participants. It will also signal your intentionality about the importance of prayer (new or ongoing) to everyone in the congregation. But the kick-off seminar can be held in March if that is when you begin. No need to wait—take the plunge!

As you will see, the only "time-sensitive" events are in November, December and May. But even those allow some flexibility. The Harp & Bowl Thanksgiving Celebration can easily become a Harp & Bowl Celebration of Thanks any other month of the year if November does not work for your church schedule. Similarly, the National Day of Prayer event would be just as effective around the 4th of July if the nationally scheduled observance is not an option for some reason. Be flexible. Incorporate the flavor, uniqueness and preferences of your own congregation as much as possible.

KEEPING THE MAIN THING THE MAIN THING

As with any push in prayer ministry, make sure your pastor is on board. Schedule a time with your pastor to share your vision and ask him to pray with you about which events are right for your congregation and how frequently they should be offered. Come well prepared to this meeting. Your pastor does not want or need additional responsibilities to shoulder. Preparation will show him that you are capable of pulling off these events with minimal requirements from the pastoral staff. Support from the pulpit and plenty of advertising through verbal announcements and/or bulletin inserts should be all that is requested of them, if possible.

If you haven't already determined your church's vision or mission statement, now is the time to do that. Every prayer event needs to have a focused, all-in-one-accord prayer thrust to make it successful. These focus topics should be areas for which your church already has a burden. Some prayer topics will be universal—prayer for our nation is an example. But maybe your church supports a missionary in Indonesia. Indonesia, then, will be a primary prayer target for you. Maybe you have developed a prison ministry or an outreach to neighborhood youth. These things must not only be incorporated into your prayer events, *they are the primary reasons your prayer events take place.* Your Prayer for the Nations event in July may morph into a Prayer for Indonesia Rally. Your Neighborhood Prayerwalk will no doubt be focused on reaching and ministering to the youth. Discuss and pinpoint these prayer thrusts with your pastor to make sure they coordinate with his vision for the church.

It goes without saying that your prayer event should be a loose framework for your invitation to the Holy Spirit to lead. Setting a rigid, inflexible schedule will be death to your event. If your schedule calls for a time of praise, confession, intercession and then listening, but you sense a move of the Holy Spirit during the confession segment that requires you stay in that mode for the rest of the evening—go with it! Don't quench what the Spirit is doing in favor of a pre-determined agenda.

Every prayer event needs to be bathed in prayer. As soon as you know something is on the schedule at your church, begin to pray for the event to reach its target audience. Pray that it will be Spirit-led and build the kingdom. These events aren't meant to be a one-time thing never to be re-visited. They are a launching point for on-going prayer ministry. The Prayer for the Nations rally is meant to encourage prayer for missions on a continued basis; the Men's Prayer Breakfast should encourage men to participate regularly in prayer, etc. Don't prayerwalk your neighborhood one time only—keep that going by periodically offering a prayerwalk in the same or new areas.

Any of these events can be as elaborate or as simple as you care to make them. Add or take away elements from the suggested schedule to fit your needs. Loosen or tighten the time frames to suit your group. Just be sure to keep the main thing, the main thing. Don't let the event dominate or overtake the purpose: prayer.

September

KICK OFF SEMINAR

Enlist and equip pray-ers by hosting a prayer seminar.

Planning a prayer seminar to launch your year of prayer events is an excellent way to get everyone on the same page regarding prayer. Most people have received little or no training in the area of prayer and feel ill-equipped and skeptical about their abilities to participate as part of a prayer team or ministry. Sad to say, seminaries are often lacking in this type of training, so even pastors are sometimes hesitant to support and commit to a ministry that they don't feel qualified to direct. A seminar that includes good basic instruction as well as vision-casting will encourage all of your church members to embrace the importance and possibilities of prayer. You will be able to build on the foundation laid at this time through future training seminars and conferences.

Essentials

If this is the first-ever prayer seminar your church has offered, it is best to start small. Don't overwhelm everyone (including yourself) with something that leaves you drained and defeated. The object is to get everyone feeling good about prayer, not ready to run in the opposite direction. Start dreaming now of hosting a multi-church prayer conference, but save that for the future when you have more experience and can better understand some of the demands this would require. Also, a multi-church conference will only work if your church and pastor has a history of doing events with other churches and relationships are already developed.

As prayer leader, you need to be sensitive to church leadership. Their support is a key ingredient for success—especially with this event. A seminar crosses over into the area of teaching and instruction which is usually the responsibility of the senior pastor. This is his territory, so make sure you address all of his concerns. Incorporate his desires and vision even if it's less than what you hoped. Don't push, but lead capably *under his authority.*

At the outset there are a few basic questions you need to ask that will help you determine the type of seminar that will best fit the needs of your church. These questions will revolve around three primary areas:

- Budget
- Speaker
- Length/Format

Budget: Bottom line—how much money do you have to spend? Your budget will dictate your options for the speaker as well as the length and format of this event. Options are truly endless, but included in this chapter are ideas for **low budget**, **modest budget** and **generous budget** scenarios.

Speaker: Based on your budget, you must decide if you will bring in an outside speaker or rely on a video seminar or other materials that will accomplish your goals. Obviously, the more you are able to put into this, the better your results. Bringing in someone who is gifted at teaching and motivating in the area of prayer (even if it is via video) will give you the edge.

Length/Format of Seminar: Your budget and speaker will determine in part the length and format of your seminar. But there are other considerations. Is it a busy time of year? How much help will you have for clean up/set up, etc.? Be realistic—you can't do this all on your own.

No matter what type of event you hold, be sure to end with some type of a challenge. Pray about what you want that to look like. Do you want to ask for volunteers for the prayer chain, prayer team or prayer room? Do you want to offer a Bible study on prayer for those who want more training or announce a new weekly prayer time? Prepare sign up sheets in advance where it is appropriate.

Sample Low Budget Model

This model assumes that "low" means that costs are coming out of your own pocket. It also assumes that no one at your church feels adequate at this time to motivate and equip on the topic of prayer. Having a multiple day event will give weight to the importance your church is putting on prayer even if prayer is not yet a budget item.

Teaching will be provided through audio tapes/CDs with break out sessions for discussion and prayer. You will need to make advance preparations for audio equipment so that all can hear adequately. The length and number of your sessions will depend on the audio materials you choose, so think that through regarding your schedule. Prepare discussion questions in advance remembering that these should reinforce what was just learned in the previous audio tape/CD session. Keep in mind that the break-out sessions are short and part of that time should be allocated to prayer. You will be providing minimal refreshments Friday evening and Saturday morning. Ask everyone to bring a brown bag lunch on Saturday.

Sample Schedule

Friday P.M.
7:00 – 7:15 Welcome everyone, open in prayer asking the Holy Spirit to capture every heart present with the importance of prayer.
Make a few opening remarks about your burden to see your church become a house of prayer.
7:15 - ? Make popcorn and soft drinks available as your group watches a motivational DVD/video (see resources at the end of this chapter for suggestions).
Have someone close in prayer reaffirming your desire to become a prayer-saturated church.

Saturday A.M.
9:00 – 9:20 Have coffee bar and donuts ready and allow everyone to fellowship as you wait for latecomers.
9:20 – 9:45 Welcome and worship.
9:45 – 10:30 Session #1: Listen to audio materials.
10:30 – 10:50 Break out in small groups to discuss and pray about

session #1 material using discussion questions prepared in advance.
10:50 – 11:00 Break
11:00 – 11:45 Session #2: Listen to audio materials.
11:45 – 12:05 Break out in small groups to discuss and pray about session #2 material using discussion questions prepared in advance.
12:05 – 12:35 Brown bag lunch break.
12:35 – 1:20 Session #3: Listen to audio materials.
1:20 – 1:45 Have everyone find a spot to get alone to go over notes and pray about what they've heard so far.
1:45 – 2:30 Session #4: Listen to audio materials.
2:30 – 3:00 Corporate worship and prayer.
Close or come back after a dinner break for another session of worship and audio materials or show another motivational video. Don't forget to leave them with a challenge and request for their commitment to get involved in prayer.

Sample Modest Budget Model

This model assumes that you have a small budget provided by the church or that you have several prayer champions in your congregation who are willing to pool resources to get the prayer ministry off the ground. This model will incorporate an actual video training seminar on the topic of prayer over multiple days.

You will need to make arrangements for video equipment that allows for everyone to be able to see adequately. Video seminars are often all-inclusive and will provide hand-out material for your participants or a master from which you will make photocopies. Usually the video itself will have you stop the tape/DVD at an appropriate time for prayer or discussion, etc.

Your potluck supper will require organizational decisions (who will bring what?) and set-up/tear-down help. The sample schedule includes a brown bag lunch break, but you may opt to serve lunch which will require additional preparation. Make sure you have adequate help.

Sample Schedule

Friday P.M.

6:00 – 6:15 Welcome everyone, open in prayer asking the Holy Spirit to capture every heart present with the importance of prayer.
Make a few opening remarks about your burden to see your church become a house of prayer.

6:15 – 7:15 Potluck supper.

7:15 – 7:35 Worship

7:35 – 8:35 Opening session. Video seminar.
(As the Holy Spirit leads, and depending on your topic for the evening, you may want to be prepared with more worship and a time of prayer ministry for those who want to come forward).
Have someone close in prayer reaffirming your desire to become a people of prayer.

Saturday A.M.

8:30 – 9:00 Serve continental breakfast.

9:00 – 9:30 Welcome and worship.

9:30 – 10:30 Session #1: Video Seminar

10:30 – 10:45 Break

10:45 – 11:45 Session #2: Video Seminar

11:45 – 12:30 Brown bag lunch break.

12:30 – 1:30 Session #3: Video Seminar

1:30 – 1:45 Break

1:45 – 2:45 Session #4: Video Seminar.
2:45 – 3:30 Corporate worship and prayer.

Close or come back after a dinner break for another session of worship and training depending on the video materials you choose. If the video seminar package contains too much material to cover in the allotted time, consider having participants return Sunday afternoon after lunch.

Don't forget to challenge them and request a commitment of some kind to get involved in prayer. If your video materials already make a point of this, reinforce the challenge given there.

Sample Generous Budget Model

If you have generous funding for this event, you are blessed! This model encourages the use of outside speakers who are gifted at motivating and training in the area of prayer. The Appendix section gives ideas on how to locate a good speaker as well as guidelines on travel expenses, honorariums, housing, meals, etc. You will be able to ask potential speakers to provide you with a preview tape/CD in advance so that you can get an idea of their style and abilities. Each speaker will have his/her own requirements for remuneration, etc., so ask plenty of questions when you make contact. Remember, speakers are usually booked well in advance, so allow adequate time to reserve a speaker for your event.

The length of your seminar will depend on your speaker's flight schedule and time available. They might need to fly in on a Friday afternoon and fly out again Saturday evening. Or they might be free to stay over through Sunday and minister in your Sunday morning church service after a Friday/Saturday seminar. Some may even require that speaking in the Sunday morning worship service be part of the weekend.

Discuss with your speaker what you hope to accomplish during this seminar including the final challenge you would like to have presented to the attendees. Coordinate ideas and schedules with them as they will already have suggestions and preferences. They've done this many times before and can eliminate a lot of concerns and decisions for you. Be sure to connect with them several times before the event to confirm flight arrivals/departures and to find out if they need any special equipment (power point projectors, video equipment, photocopies made, etc.).

Sample Schedule

A sample schedule for the **generous budget** model would be similar to the **modest budget** model suggestions utilizing a live speaker rather than a video seminar for the sessions. As mentioned, the schedule will be dependant, of course, on the needs/preferences of the speaker you select.

Don't Forget!

- ☑ Critical: Provide plenty of prayer coverage well in advance of your event!
- ☑ Coordinate date, time and use of meeting space with church office. Make sure your event does not conflict with other events. If you are holding a multiple-day event, be sure you leave time for clean up, etc. If there is a wedding scheduled at 7:00 p.m. and your seminar

is done at 3:00 p.m., don't assume that will work. The event following yours will require prep and set-up time that could be a conflict.

- ☑ Promote your event! In addition to bulletin inserts, power point and verbal announcements and inclusion on the church calendar, personal promotion will encourage participation.
- ☑ Make arrangements for food: preparation, service and clean-up.
- ☑ Prepare for speaker/video in advance. If using video or audio materials, arrange for special equipment if needed. Arrange for any resources your speaker requires.
- ☑ Prepare discussion point/questions for break out groups if required.
- ☑ If you bring in an outside speaker, be sure all travel, housing and meal arrangements are made.
- ☑ Prepare sign up sheets if needed attached to 3 or 4 clipboards to circulate (attach a pen or pencil to the clipboard).

Hint: Consider ending your seminar with a Concert of Prayer (see August event for help); if you have an outside speaker, invite area churches to join you for this portion of the event.

Resources

Speakers: See Appendix for guidelines and list of possible speakers.

Motivational Videos: The Sentinel Group offers several excellent motivational videos/DVDs. *Transformation I, Transformation II, Let the Seas Resound,* and *An Unconventional War* are available at www.sentinelgroup.com.

Audio tapes/CD Prayer Training: Eddie & Alice Smith with the U.S. Prayer Center have audio cassettes available at www.prayerbookstore.com. *A Prayer Enrichment* audio cassette seminar by Albert Lemmons can be found at www.prayershop.org. The Church Prayer Leaders Network has DVDs and CDs of past conferences available at www.prayershop.org.

Video Prayer Seminars: Every Home for Christ offers a video seminar on *Practical Prayer* as well as their *Change the World School of Prayer.* www.ehc.org. U.S. Prayer Center has video materials at www.prayerbookstore.org. Renewal Ministries offers *Acts 29 Prayer Encounter* video series at www.prayerpointpress.com.

Notes

Notes

October

PRAYERWALK

Switch the month if October weather isn't ideal where you live—otherwise, what a great way to enjoy the autumn colors!

Prayerwalking is simply praying with purpose as you walk. The object of this event is to take your group to a specific location in order to offer up prayers for that area that will be more insightful and direct. It is also an excellent exercise in listening for God's voice as it requires all of your senses to be tuned to Him for His leading.

The biblical roots behind prayerwalking are found in Luke 10 when Jesus appointed 72 of His followers to go out in pairs to prepare the way for Him to come. The first thing they were to do was say, "Peace to this house" (v. 5). They were to minister and declare the nearness of God's kingdom as they went. In a very real way, prayerwalking prepares the way for the gospel to come to an area through blessing and observant, Spirit-led ministry through prayer.

Essentials

Select an area to prayerwalk. The most obvious area would be the neighborhood around your church, but feel free to walk another area if desired. Encourage participants to wear comfortable walking shoes, a watch, and dress appropriately for the weather. A small pocket Bible, a little notebook and pen, and prayer guides will be useful. Bottled water might be s5omething you want to consider providing for the participants.

Make sure everyone is safe. Break up into groups—families can walk together, or people can team up in twos or threes, but make sure no one goes out alone. If you are prayerwalking a questionable neighborhood, make sure your groups go out and return during daylight hours and that women are always escorted by men for protection. Use cell phones to be able to stay in contact. Decide ahead of time which group will cover which areas, how long you will walk, and where you will meet afterward. Be considerate of your group—keep in mind the age and health issues represented. It's best not to start out with a five-mile trek!

Have your group meet at the appointed time and place for a briefing. Explain the concept, areas to be walked, and hand out prayer guides if you have them. Give examples of things to look for: if you hear people yelling as you pass by, pray for peace in that home. If a house looks run down and unkempt, pray for finances and hope to come to that family. Be as inconspicuous as possible as you introduce the Holy Spirit's activity into the area. As He guides you, pray, bless and declare God's Word to tear down strongholds that keep people from Christ.

The debriefing at the end of your event should allow time for people to share what they saw and what they felt led to pray. If something strikes you as extremely significant to the health of your church, be flexible and pray about it together as a group. You might consider starting a journal so that future prayerwalkers in this area will be able to build on what was prayed previously.

Sample Schedules

Saturday A.M.

10:00 Meet at church

10:00 – 10:30 Discuss prayerwalking concepts

Divide area to be walked among participants. Commission the prayerwalk in prayer asking the Holy Spirit to guide you.

10:30 – 11:30 Prayerwalk assigned areas

11:30 Meet back at church

11:30 – 12:00 Debrief – Allow people to share their experiences and what they were led to pray. This can be done over lunch or refreshments (optional), but at least make water available.

Close in prayer.

Alternate Sunday Schedule

12:00 noon Meet after Sunday services

Have everyone bring a sack lunch or have something simple like pizza to eat as you discuss prayerwalking concepts.

Divide area to be walked among participants.

Commission the prayerwalk in prayer asking the Holy Spirit to guide you.

12:30 – 1:30 Prayerwalk assigned areas

1:30 Meet back at church

1:30 – 2:00 Debrief – Allow people to share their experiences and what they were led to pray. Serve beverages (optional) or make water available.

Close in prayer.

Don't Forget!

- ☑ Give adequate prayer coverage prior to the event.
- ☑ Coordinate date, time and use of meeting space with church office. Make sure your event does not conflict with other events. Trying to hold a prayerwalk on the same day that the church softball league has a game might not be the best choice.
- ☑ Promote your event! Put it in the bulletin, use power point and announce from the pulpit at least two weeks in advance (three if possible). Be sure to get it on the church calendar if you have one.
- ☑ Select areas to be prayerwalked in advance.
- ☑ Remind participants to wear comfortable walking shoes and appropriate weather gear.
- ☑ Provide prayer guides/prompts.
- ☑ Purchase and record information in a prayer journal, if desired.
- ☑ Make arrangements for refreshments or beverages if served. At least provide water for the participants.

Hint: If the weather suddenly turns bad, consider prayer-walking a local mall.

Resources

Prayerwalking: Praying On-Site with Insight by Steve Hawthorne and Graham Kendrick is an excellent handbook. It is available along with other information on prayerwalking and prayerwalking tools at www.waymakers.org. *Paths of Gold* is a handy, pocket-sized

Scriptural guide for praying for the lost. Go to www.praymag.com. Most of these products are also available at www.prayershop.org.

Notes

November

Harp & Bowl Thanksgiving Celebration

Enjoy a blend of worship and prayer as You thank God for what He's done!

". . . celebrate His lovely name with music."
(Ps. 135:3, NLT)

The Thanksgiving Celebration offers an opportunity for your group to spend time in corporate prayer thanking God for things He has done rather than making requests of Him. Harp & Bowl refers to a prayer style that alternates between spoken prayers and worship songs with some type of worship accompaniment played softly in the background throughout.

The idea of Harp & Bowl intercession comes from the symbolism in Rev. 5:8-9: "The four living creatures and the 24 elders fell down before the Lamb. Each one had a harp and they were holding golden bowls full of incense, which are the prayers of the saints. And they sang a new song: 'You are worthy to take the scroll and to open its seals, because you were slain, and with your blood you purchased men for God from every tribe and language and people and nation.'" In this passage, the harps (symbolizing worship) are combined with bowls full of incense (the prayers of the saints). These verses go on to explain why this prayer style lends itself well to a Thanksgiving Celebration: the new song that resulted in heaven centered on Christ's worthiness because of the things He has done for us. (See the resources section that follows for further reading on the theology behind Harp & Bowl.)

Harp & Bowl is not limited to thanksgiving, however. It is an exciting and enjoyable way to intercede as well. This event will encourage you and your congregation to incorporate more of this style into the prayer life of your church.

Essentials

Obviously, music is a key factor in the Harp & Bowl prayer style. Coordinating the event with your worship team well in advance will make things flow smoothly. Select worship songs that focus on what God has done for us. Your worship team will need to lead in worship intermittently and segue into soft background music during the spoken prayer intervals. NOTE: it is possible to achieve this Harp & Bowl prayer style even if you do not have a worship team and are forced to use CDs. It will take practice and someone who is vigilant on the CD player, but it is possible.

The spoken prayer portion can be handled numerous ways

depending on the "freedom" your people have in public prayer. Be sensitive to this. Don't imagine that people who have never prayed publicly will suddenly become seasoned intercessors in front of the microphone. If your people are experienced pray-ers, open the microphone for different ones to lead out in prayer. Remind them to keep the prayer focus on giving thanks. It is wise with any prayer event to ask several people in advance to be prepared to participate in leading prayer. That way there will not be prolonged periods of uncomfortable silence. Some silence is fine—even preferable at times. But if no one participates it will be awkward, so think ahead. Adjust the schedule to fit your needs with longer/shorter prayer and worship segments and length of service as needed.

The finale to this Thanksgiving Celebration will be the responsive reading of your corporate "church psalm" (patterned after Ps. 136). In preparation for this, pass out slips of paper at the beginning of your event and ask people to write a short sentence of thanks for something that God has done in your church or for members of the congregation during the past year. Give them an opportunity to think about it during the first segment and then collect the slips of paper for the psalm leader (see schedule). Depending on the size of your group, many of the slips will be duplicates. During the event, the psalm leader should sort through and group the responses so that each item is read only once. The psalm leader will read one of the submitted statements of thanks and the congregation will respond in unison continuing through all the expressions of thanks. Begin as Psalm 136 begins and then switch to the specific items of thanks for your church as in the following example:

PSALM LEADER: Give thanks to the Lord, for He is good.

UNISON: His love endures forever.

PSALM LEADER: Give thanks to the God of gods:
UNISON: His love endures forever.
PSALM LEADER: Give thanks to the Lord of lords:
UNISON: His love endures forever.
PSALM LEADER: to him who alone does great wonders,
UNISON: His love endures forever.
PSALM LEADER: who by his understanding made the heavens,
UNISON: His love endures forever.
PSALM LEADER: He brought ten new families to us this year.
UNISON: His love endures forever.
PSALM LEADER: He healed Pastor Bob's back.
UNISON: His love endures forever.
PSALM LEADER: Three children received Christ in Sunday school.
UNISON: His love endures forever.

Continue . . .

Sample Schedule

P.M.

Pre-prep Make slips of paper available on every seat.

7:00 – 7:15 Open with a brief explanation of the evening's focus: thanksgiving.

Ask everyone to write out a short sentence of thanks for something God has done for the church or its members this year.

Read Scripture passages: Rev. 5:8-9 and Ps. 50:23.

Open in prayer asking God to accept this evening of thanksgiving as a sweet smelling offering.

7:15 – 7:25 Worship songs

7:25 – 7:30 Open up time for spoken prayers of thanks at microphone with music playing softly in background.

7:30 – 7:35 Collect slips of paper and give to the psalm leader as the worship team leads a worship song.

7:35 – 7:40 Open up time for spoken prayers of thanks with music playing softly in background. Invite families to stand together and lead in prayer at microphone.

7:40 – 7:45 Worship song

7:45 – 7:55 Open up time for spoken prayer of thanks with music playing softly in background. Invite sentence prayers from people right at their seats.

7:50 – 7:55 Worship song

7:55 – 8:00 Read Scripture: 1 Chron. 29:10-14

8:00 – ? Psalm leader reads psalm (see instructions and previous sample) with congregation responding in unison.

Close in prayer.

Refreshments (optional)

Don't Forget!

- ☑ Critical: Provide plenty of prayer coverage well in advance of your event!
- ☑ Coordinate date, time and use of meeting space with church office. Make sure your event does not conflict with other events. **Planning an event like this over the Thanksgiving holiday when people are out of town might not be the best choice. Consider the Sunday evening prior to Thanksgiving.**
- ☑ Promote your event! Put it in the bulletin, use power point and announce from the pulpit at least two weeks

in advance (three, if possible). Be sure to get it on the church calendar if you have one.

- ☑ Select music and work with worship team in advance.
- ☑ Be flexible on the time allotted to music and prayer—go with the flow.
- ☑ Ask several people to be prepared to pray prayers of thanks.
- ☑ Provide slips of paper for event finale.
- ☑ Make arrangements for refreshments if served.

Hint: It's always good to come prepared with selected passages of Scripture to read if prayer times lag. Appropriate ones might include: Psalms 33, 100, 103, 111.

Resources

Harp & Bowl theology: Articles on Harp & Bowl intercession are available at www.praymag.com in the online archives: "Pray It with Song" by Dick Eastman; "The Tabernacle of David" by Mike Bickle; "The Two Essentials of Devotion" by Ross Parsley; "International House of Prayer" by Mike Bickle.

Further reading: Dick Eastman's *Delight Trilogy (Heights of Delight, Pathways of Delight* and *Rivers of Delight)* is part of the Harp & Bowl series from Regal Books. It is available at www.ehc.org. For in-depth study, Mike Bickle offers a three part syllabus on the Harp & Bowl movement at www.fotb.org.

Notes

Notes

December

Advent Prayers

A prayerful look at Jesus, Mary and Joseph, the Shepherds and the Magi.

This prayer event adds a new prayer dimension to your church's Advent celebration or allows you to begin a new tradition. Advent is the period of waiting and preparation prior to the birth of Christ. It begins on the fourth Sunday prior to Christmas day. Traditionally, the celebration of Advent involves the lighting of one candle each Sunday accompanied by a reading or lesson on some aspect of the nativity story.

This prayer-focused version of the Advent celebration includes a coordinated weekly prayer focus for families to participate in at home during the season leading up to Christmas.

Essentials

As always, you will need the consent and blessing of your pastor for any prayer event. However, since this event is on-going throughout the Christmas season and is intended to be a portion of the main Sunday worship service, it is especially important to work hand in hand with church leadership. Work with them far enough in advance so that they can incorporate this prayer focus into the other elements of your church's busy holiday season.

Little is required in the way of preparation. You will need to provide an evergreen wreath with four candles for the front of the church and be prepared to read (or have someone else read) the Scripture and prayer provided in this chapter. Make copies of the weekly prayer program included here for each one in your congregation. That way they will be able to read along, respond at the appropriate place, and take it home with them to use as a prayer-focused devotional each day throughout the week.

Begin on the fourth Sunday before Christmas. The first week, the candles remain unlit until the prayer leader comes forward to read the Scripture and say the prayer—then the *first candle only* will be lighted. The next Sunday, light the first candle *prior to the start of the service* and then light the second one during the Scripture and prayer. Each week add the lighting of an additional candle until all four have been lighted. Be sure to explain that the weekly prayer focus is being provided so that everyone can be meditating on the same Scriptures and prayer prompts throughout the week. Encourage them to take it home and make it a part of their Christmas festivities.

You may find your pastor enthusiastic enough to prepare sermons around each week's Advent theme in which case the weekly prayer focus will have the congregation meditating and praying the sermon points each day.

Advent Prayers

Week One – Jesus went to Bethlehem out of love.

Prayer Leader:

Read – Jn. 1:1-14; Jn. 3:16

Prayer: *Our Lord Jesus Christ, Creator of the world, we bless Your Name! We truly cannot conceive of Your sacrifice as You left heaven. You stepped down from absolute control to a place of absolute dependence as a baby. To humble Yourself in such a way—to be vulnerable to the mistakes and frailties of earthly caregivers and then to lay down Your life for us—causes us to stand amazed at Your selfless expression of love. May we follow Your lead and show the same kind of love to those around us; may we love to the point of sacrifice.*

Congregational Response: *Not our will, but Your's be done.*

Weekly Prayer Focus: (Use these Scriptures and thoughts to prompt meditation and prayer throughout the week).

Monday: Lord, teach us to love *sacrificially* (Jn. 15:13; Jn. 3:16).

Tuesday: Lord, help us to love *unconditionally* (Rom. 5:8, 8:38-39).

Wednesday: Lord, teach us to love *incarnationally* (Phil. 2:5-8; Jn. 1:14).

Thursday: Lord, may we learn to love *without measure* (Eph. 3:17-19).

Friday: Lord, instruct us to love *perfectly* (1 Cor. 13).

Saturday: Lord, teach us to *receive* Your love (Jn. 1:12; Rom. 10:9-10).

Week Two – Mary and Joseph went to Bethlehem out of obedience.

Prayer Leader:

Read – Lk. 1:26-55; Mt. 18:24

Prayer: *Father, we thank You for Your elaborate plan of salvation, conceived before time began as the ultimate rescue mission to ransom us from destruction. Thank You for the willingness of Mary and Joseph to embrace what You were doing and face humiliation and rejection to see Your kingdom come to earth. May we seek to have the same kind of faith and humility as these two Jewish young people as we make ourselves available to You no matter what the cost.*

Congregational Response: *Be it unto us as You have said.*

Weekly Prayer Focus: (Use these Scriptures and thoughts to prompt meditation and prayer throughout the week).

Monday: Lord, may we always do *what You require* (Micah 6:8).

Tuesday: Lord, teach us be *humble* (Jas. 4:10).

Wednesday: Lord, show us how to have *faith* (Rom. 5:1; Heb. 11:6).

Thursday: Lord, help us to *follow* Your ways (Ps. 25:4-5; Jn. 14:15).

Friday: Lord, may we be willing to face *rejection* (Jn. 15:20, 16:33; Lk. 6:22).

Saturday: Lord, teach us to *lay down our lives* (Lk. 9:23-24).

Week Three – The Shepherds went to Bethlehem out of awe.

Prayer Leader:

Read – Lk. 2:8-20

Prayer: *Lord of hosts, thank You for revealing Your unspeakable gift to shepherds on a hillside. Thank You for lighting up the sky with Your declaration of peace. Thank You for inviting them—and us—to come to the manger to see the Word made flesh. You entrusted Your simple message to simple people so that we would know that Your salvation is for everyone. May we always turn aside to see when You are trying to show us something. May our faith make us willing to leave everything to follow You.*

Congregational Response: *Let us go see this thing which the Lord told us about.*

Weekly Prayer Focus: (Use these Scriptures and thoughts to prompt meditation and prayer throughout the week).

Monday: Lord, may we always turn aside to *hear Your voice* (Ex. 3:4; Jn. 10:27).

Tuesday: Lord, make us into good soil to *receive Your Word* (Mk. 4:13-20).

Wednesday: Lord, help us to *believe* (Mk. 9:24; Jn. 6:29, 9:35-38, 20:29).

Thursday: Lord, teach us to leave everything to *follow You* (Lk. 9:61-62).

Friday: Lord, may we learn to *love Your Word* (Ps. 119:97,140; Jer. 15:16).

Saturday: Lord, help us to *declare Your Word* (Rom. 10:13-15; Eph. 6:19-20).

Week Four – The Magi went to Bethlehem out of devotion.

Prayer Leader:

Read – Mt. 2:1-14

Prayer: *King of kings, You revealed Your coming in ancient texts and wrote it in the sky for all to see. Thank You for inviting the Wiseman from the East so that we would know that Your salvation is for wise and simple, rich and poor, Jew and Gentile. Thank You for presenting the complexities of Your plan in such a way that learned scholars traveled across the world to see the unfolding of wisdom foretold in the universe. May we study Your Word and seek You out—may we always pursue Your truth out of sheer devotion.*

Congregational Response: *We have come to worship Him.*

Weekly Prayer Focus: (Use these Scriptures and thoughts to prompt meditation and prayer throughout the week).

Monday: Lord, show us how to *seek* You (Ps. 119:10; Jer. 29:12-13).

Tuesday: Lord, help us to *follow hard* after You (Deut. 30:19; Ps. 111:10).

Wednesday: Lord, teach us to *worship* You (Jn. 4:23).

Thursday: Lord, instruct us to *watch for signs* of Your presence (Ex. 33:7-10).

Friday: Lord, let us always *enjoy* Your presence (Ps. 16:22, 27:4).

Saturday: Lord, may we learn to *appreciate* You for who You are (Phil. 2:9-11).

Hint: It would be a special touch to pre-select families or children to come to the front each week to light a candle as the Scripture is read and prayer is said.

Don't Forget!

- ☑ Critical: Provide plenty of prayer coverage well in advance of your event!
- ☑ Coordinate this event with your pastor. Be sure this will work into his schedule for your church's holiday celebration.
- ☑ Provide a wreath and candles (and lighters or matches) for the front of the church.
- ☑ In advance, select someone to be the reader and candle lighter each week.
- ☑ Make copies of the prayer program for each person in the congregation.

Resources

You have permission to reproduce as many copies of the Advent Prayers as needed for your church prayer event. Use the following credit line: Taken from *A Year of Prayer Events for Your Church*, PrayerShop Publishing, © 2007, used by permission.

Notes

January

Pray through Your Building

Create an atmosphere of blessing by praying through your church building.

". . . May there be no enemy breaking through our walls, no going into captivity" (Ps. 144:14, NLT)

The concept behind praying through your church building is similar to the idea behind prayerwalking. You are preparing the way for the presence of the Lord through blessing and intercession. Many churches have teams that pray through their building on a regular basis throughout the year. Some even do it weekly as a way of preparing for the services on Sunday.

This building-pray-through event is a low-key version of a church cleansing. If you sense that there are issues going on in your church that must be resolved through spiritual warfare, you will need to do additional homework before planning that type of full-fledged cleansing event. Resources at the end of this chapter will direct you to reading that can help. Understanding issues such as spiritual mapping will enable you to determine some of the footholds that have been given to the enemy.

Essentials

Your group will meet at the appointed time for a briefing and then divide up into groups to cover the area more efficiently. You will find that there are people who naturally have a heart for certain ministries that are represented by different areas of the church. It is fine to let those people be responsible to cover those areas. But make sure you have all areas covered—don't leave any gaps. Choose a time when the church is unoccupied so that you aren't forced to work around areas being used. This may mean you have to be creative in selecting a time to schedule this event.

As you walk through the building, be aware of all that the Holy Spirit is pointing out to you. Pray for the people and ministries you know occupy each area. You will find an endless number of prayer prompts to keep you going. Certain areas will represent certain things, so pray specifically for what takes place there (or what you *want* to take place there). In the foyer pray for the newcomers to feel welcomed. In the sanctuary pray over each chair or pew and the people who will be sitting in them; pray for the pulpit and the word that goes out from it, the musician's instruments and the worship team that uses them, etc.

Here are some suggestions for areas to be covered in prayer. Be sure to adjust the list to fit your own church building:

- Foyer
- Sanctuary
- Pastor(s) Office(s)
- Sunday School Rooms
- Nursery Rooms
- Kitchen
- Fellowship Hall
- Youth Hall or Gym
- Prayer Room
- Outside Perimeter of Building
- Parking Lot

As with the prayerwalk, explain the concept, areas to be covered, and hand out prayer guides if you have them. Encourage everyone to listen to the promptings of the Holy Spirit and ask for His direction and wisdom. If someone feels impressed to pray in the furnace room, for instance, and it isn't "on the list"—by all means, cover it adequately in prayer. If you ask for wisdom, you must believe that you will receive it and pray responsively (Jas. 1:5-8). Once you've prayed through the building, end with a debriefing allowing time for people to share what they felt led to pray. If something strikes you as extremely significant to the health of your church, go back to that area and pray about it together as a larger group. Ask the Lord if deeper prayer work needs to be done. You may discover after this initial pray-through that a more thorough spiritual cleansing should be scheduled for a later date.

Sample Schedules

Saturday A.M.

10:00 Meet at church.

10:00 – 10:30 Discuss concepts.

Divide area to be covered among participants.

Commission the building pray-through in prayer asking the Holy Spirit to guide.

10:30 – 11:30 Pray through assigned areas.

11:30 Meet back at specified location.

11:30 – 12:00 Debrief – Allow people to share their experiences and what they were led to pray. This can be done over lunch or refreshments (optional).

Closing prayer.

Alternate Sunday Schedule

12:00 noon Meet after Sunday services.

Have everyone bring a sack lunch or provide something easy such as pizza to eat as you discuss walk-through concepts.

Divide area to be covered among participants.

Commission the building pray-through in prayer asking the Holy Spirit to guide.

12:30 – 1:30 Pray through assigned areas.

1:30 Meet back at specified location.

1:30 – 2:00 Debrief – Allow people to share their experiences and what they were led to pray. Serve beverages (optional).

Closing prayer.

Don't Forget!

- ☑ Prepare for your building pray-through with adequate pre-event prayer coverage.
- ☑ Coordinate date, time and use of the church building with church office. Make sure your event does not conflict with other events. Remember to choose a time when the *entire* building is unoccupied.
- ☑ Promote your event! Put it in the bulletin, use power point and announce from the pulpit at least two weeks in advance (three if possible). Be sure to get it on the church calendar if you have one. **Note:** When doing a more thorough spiritual cleansing, you will want to select a team of intercessors with an understanding of spiritual warfare to be involved rather than opening it up to the entire church.
- ☑ Determine all the areas to be covered in advance.
- ☑ Provide prayer guides.
- ☑ Make arrangements for refreshments or beverages if served.

Hint: Consider repeating this event multiple times a year—just as you would clean your house more than once every 12 months.

Resources

Waymakers has specific prayer prompt material for praying blessings over an area at www.waymakers.org. A variety of helpful prayer guides including "Life-Giving Prayers for Your Church" are available at www.prayershop.org.

Additional reading regarding spiritual cleansing of your church: *The Devil Goes to Church* by Dave Butts is available at www.prayershop.org. The May 2006 issue of Empowered was on the topic of spiritual cleansing your church. You may review articles at http://new.prayerleader.com/content/blogcategory/39/23/.

Spiritual Mapping: The Sentinel Group offers an audio series called *Unleashing the Power of Informed Intercession* at www.sentinelgroup.org. Eddie and Alice Smith offer several resources regarding spiritual warfare/mapping at www.prayerbookstore.com. While these resources may be focused on spiritual mapping of a city or country, the principles will apply to mapping any area including your church.

Notes

Notes

February

NIGHTWATCH PRAYER VIGIL

A sleep-fasting, nighttime format for seeking God.

"Praise the LORD, all you servants of the LORD who minister by night in the house of the LORD. Lift up your hands in the sanctuary and praise the LORD." (Ps. 134:1-2, NLT)

A nightwatch can be held for various reasons: prayer coverage for an important upcoming event, praying through in instances of extreme desperation, or during a time when your church wants to hear the Lord's voice on an important decision. Jesus spent entire nights alone communing with God (Lk. 6:12), and we have an example of the church meeting all night for prayer when Peter was imprisoned (Acts 12:5-18). We are using a *seek and soak* format for the model given here: seeking the Lord's presence and then lingering there.

Watching during the night hours is a wonderful way to help people "press in" as they pray. Since it occurs at a time when run-of-the-mill meetings aren't typically scheduled, and attendees are fasting sleep in order to attend, it creates its own atmosphere of priority and expectation. Obviously, this won't be for everyone, and many will doubt if they can spend a whole night in prayer. But once they've attended and succeeded, they'll have a sense of satisfaction and accomplishment that encourages them to keep seeking and soaking in His presence.

Much of this all-nighter will be given to meditation and opportunities for personal interaction with the Lord. This is an ideal time to train your participants to expand their understanding of what prayer actually is. Prayer is relationship. It involves making requests of God—yes. He tells us to ask Him for our daily bread and says that we don't have because we don't ask. But prayer is so much more than that. Prayer is listening and communing and worshiping. It is enjoying God and allowing Him to enjoy us.

Essentials

Preparation for this event requires pulling together some or all of the resources listed to provide springboards to help your participants jump into connecting and communing. Many people have never attempted these types of activities, so prepare as if all of your attendees are novices. Even seasoned pray-ers will enjoy revisiting praise and seeking prompts they have used in the past.

Provide handouts to participants a week prior to the event asking them to bring as desired: a Bible; notebook and pen; worship CDs and player with headphones; blanket, sleeping bag or exercise mat; power bars or personal snacks; water bottle. Encourage them to wear comfortable, relaxed clothing. Explain that the event will not begin until 8:30 p.m. and that they might want to nap prior to coming. This is NOT an event for children, so people will need to know in advance that they will have to make child care arrangements.

Food at this event is not encouraged, but you'll want to provide plenty of coffee and tea (juice would be a nice touch) on hand for those who want it. Ending with a continental breakfast is certainly an option you might want to weigh; however, by that time in the morning, people are usually anxious to get home and catch up on some sleep.

Depending on the amount of room you have in your church building, you may want to set up separate rooms for different activities during the times of personal meditation. In one room you might want to have a DVD player set up to play continuously repeated showings of the *Jesus* video or *The Passion of the Christ.* This will run all night so that people can drop in to watch all or a portion as they meditate on Jesus' love and sacrifice. Another room could be set up with worship CDs playing constantly for those who don't have their own CD player and headphones. Another room might have a CD of the names of God playing continuously (see resources). Consider having another room set up for people who want to pray together aloud, etc. These rooms should have chairs placed around the perimeter or in rows according to use.

You'll also want to prepare in advance several different handouts for your participants that give them "food for thought" as they spend time interacting with God. The resource section provides information on where these can be found, but you will need to reproduce the lists for your attendees abiding by copyright guidelines given:

- 600 Names of Jesus
- Jehovah's Names

- Who I Am in Christ
- Armor of God
- Prayer Postures

You may want to collect and supply devotional materials for your participants to "check out" and return for a portion of the evening. Some suggestions are listed in the resource section, but you will probably have favorites of your own that you'll want to include. Word of warning when loaning out any materials—they may not all come back to you, so accept that ahead of time and decide if this is something you want to offer.

When your participants arrive, encourage them to find a "spot" to call their own. Some corner or section of the auditorium, lobby, etc. where they can spread out their belongings and get comfortable. The blanket, sleeping bag or exercise mat you encouraged them to bring is for times when they want to stretch out prostrate before the Lord or sit quietly by themselves—or rest!

This sample schedule calls for a time of self-examination (personal confession) and communion. This model encourages a communion table to be set up off to the side in the auditorium. Play music softly in the background as participants are given a time to examine their hearts before God. Invite them to come up to the communion table to serve themselves when they are ready. Be sure to be sensitive to the traditions your church embraces, getting permission where necessary or using a different model.

After communion, this schedule calls for a time of approaching Jesus. Meet in an area where chairs can be formed into a large circle (use multiple circular rows to accommodate the number of participants present). In the center of the circle, place a single chair.

After everyone is seated in the circle, read Matthew 18:20:

"For where two or three are gathered together in my name, there am I in the midst of them." Impress upon your group the reality of Jesus being right there in the middle—the chair representing where He is seated. Invite them to close their eyes and picture Him seated there in whatever biblical form they personally relate to. Do they see Him as a Shepherd or a King? Maybe they see Him with a group of children surrounding Him. Or maybe they "see" Him laying His hands on their head to heal them. However they see Him, ask them to place themselves in that scenario with Him. If they see themselves as one of the children, invite them to climb up in His lap. Or maybe they see themselves breaking open an alabaster box to anoint His feet, or putting their finger in the scars in His hands. Ask your participants to begin silently praying/interacting with Him from that heart place of worship. Don't cut this time short—allow the Holy Spirit to work, and it will be very meaningful.

In the wee hours of the morning, you will be inviting them to write a letter to Jesus about the night they just spent with Him: the things they thought about Him, the emotions (or lack of) they experienced. When they are finished, have them draw a line at the end of their letter and then begin to write what they "hear" Jesus saying to them. Have them start that section with: "Dear ________ (insert their name), *I love you*." Have them continue to write what they are impressed that Jesus is speaking to their hearts.

The schedule provided here is in segments so that you can use all or part as desired. If you decide to offer the full event, it provides an easy exit point at midnight for those who just aren't up to staying through the night.

Sample Schedule

Friday P.M.

8:30 – 9:00 Have coffee/beverage bar ready. As each attendee arrives, hand them a schedule of events with ideas for meditation/prayer. Give them an opportunity to "find their spot" to spread out their belongings before coming together in the main area for worship.

9:00 – 9:30 Welcome everyone. Open with prayer inviting the Holy Spirit's presence as you seek Him.

Worship.

9:30 – 10:15 Private heart preparation and communion as worship music continues.

10:15 – 10:30 Break.

10:30 – 10:45 Worship songs.

10:45 – 11:45 Approaching Jesus (empty chair in center of circle).

11:45 – 12:00 Break and good-byes to those who have to leave.

A.M.

12:00 – 12:15 Describe the various rooms you have prepared for them to use as they interact with the Lord. Explain that they are free to come and go from those as they please. They should know that the rest of the time is loosely structured. While you will be making suggested focus areas to keep it flowing, they should not feel forced to redirect their attention if they are in the middle of communing with the Lord on a different topic. Encourage them to use every prayer posture listed on the handout at least once during the evening (if they are physically able).

12:15 – 1:15 Focus: *Jehovah's Names; 600 Names of Jesus*

1:15 – 2:00 Focus: Who I Am in Christ

2:00 – 2:15 Break

2:15 – 3:00 Armor of God
3:00 – 4:00 Corporate prayer. Explain *"Keep Moving"* format (see resource section).
4:00 – 5:00 Letter to Jesus.
5:00 Dismiss with closing prayer.
Continental breakfast optional.

Hint: Don't force anyone to participate in any part of the evening which makes them feel uncomfortable. The Holy Spirit is very personal in the way He approaches each of us, so be sensitive to what He is doing and don't quench Him.

Don't Forget!

- ☑ Critical: Provide plenty of prayer coverage well in advance of your event!
- ☑ Coordinate date, time and use of meeting space with church office. Make sure your event does not conflict with other events. Don't plan this on a Saturday night or everyone will sleep through church!
- ☑ Promote your event! Use bulletin inserts, power point and verbal announcements, posters and inclusion on the church calendar.
- ☑ Make arrangements for coffee/beverage bar (and optional continental breakfast): preparation, service and clean-up.
- ☑ Make arrangements for music/worship.
- ☑ Prepare resource handouts and "break out" rooms.

Collect DVDs, CDs, and devotional materials you want to

have on hand. Provide all needed players and equipment. You may need to provide several boxes of tissues for the Approaching Jesus prayer circle.

Resources

Jehovah's Names and 600 Names of Jesus: available to download and be used for prayer training in your church context as long as the copyright and website address remains printed on it: Copyright 2006. All rights reserved. No portion of this may be copied, filed, or republished in any form without the express and written consent of the author Richard W. LaFountain. www.prayertoday.org.

Who I Am in Christ and Armor of God: see Appendices C and D. Permission is granted to reproduce as needed with copyright listed.

Information on prayer postures and "keep moving" corporate prayer format: "Body Language: Praying with Your Whole Self" by David Trembley; "Keep Moving" by Sandra Higley. Articles available in *Pray!* magazine's online archives: www.praymag.com. *Pray!* magazine gives blanket permission for up to 100 copies to be made for church use. Include the following credit on the first page: "Used by permission of *Pray!*. Copyright © 1999 ("Body Language") 2002 ("Keep Moving"), The Navigators. Used by permission of NavPress. All rights reserved."

I AM: 365 Names, Characteristics and Attributes of God: CD available at www.prayershop.org.

Devotionals: So many are available, but two suggestions would be *A Celebration of Praise* by Dick Eastman (www.ehc.org), *My Utmost for His Highest* by Oswald Chambers.

Notes

Notes

March

Prayer Initiative

Experience the unity and blessing of an all-church multi-day prayer initiative.

"Harmony is as precious as the anointing oil that was poured over Aaron's head . . . and there the Lord has pronounced his blessing." (Ps. 133:2-3, NLT)

An all-church prayer initiative allows an entire congregation to pray on the same topic for the same length of time. Similar to the weekly focused Advent Prayers supplied in the chapter for December, but with more substance, a prayer initiative can be held on any topic for any length of time you desire. Typically, prayer initiatives are held for 40 days, but you can start out with a seven, 21 or 30-day time frame if you prefer.

If your church has an upcoming evangelism outreach, a stewardship campaign for a new building project or other strategic event, it is a perfect time to launch an all-church prayer initiative as preparation for and prayer support behind this critical time in your church. But prayer initiatives have such a positive spiritual impact on your church, you may not want to wait until such an event occurs.

Prayer initiatives, more than any other event, will give your church a sense of what it means to be a house of prayer. Everyone is singularly focused, praying together with unity and purpose. You will sense God's blessing after praying together and stir up interest among potential intercessors as you go.

Essentials

A prayer initiative is not difficult to plan. There are many ongoing prayer initiatives that you can plug into just by purchasing the materials (information is listed in the resources section that follows). If, however, you decide to plan your own initiative as preparation and prayer support for an event at your church, you will need a person of prayer who listens to God's voice and is willing to prepare the daily prayer targets for everyone to use throughout the time period.

This event, as with others, will require your pastor to be supportive from the pulpit. It is extremely helpful for your pastor to speak on the topic to be covered at the outset and to continue to refer to it throughout the duration of the initiative. Some churches have had their pastor's participation to the point where he continued to speak on the topic each Sunday throughout the designated time, turning the prayer points into a sermon outline.

Sample Schedule

Sunday

Day 1: Announce from the platform that the initiative is being launched. Your pastor should support the initiative from the pulpit or cover the topic in his sermon to get people involved. Hand out the materials to everyone who plans to participate (your pastor will need to encourage full participation as this is an all-church event).

Day 1-7: Congregation prays through material at home.

Day 8: Pastor preaches on what has been covered so far or continues his support from the pulpit. If possible have a few people share testimonies of what the prayer focus has meant to them thus far.

Day 8-?: Congregation continues to pray through material at home for duration of the initiative with weekly support from the pulpit.

Last Day: Hold a prayer rally where people have a chance to share what they heard/how they were impressed during this time. This is optional, of course, but important if you are holding your prayer initiative for a specific purpose such as a stewardship drive for a building campaign. Make sure everyone has an opportunity to share any insights they received in prayer during the preceding days. End with a time of corporate prayer and worship.

Hint: Some prepared prayer initiatives have materials for children as well as adults.

Don't Forget!

☑ A prayer initiative needs to be planned well in advance (a minimum of three months). For help in planning www.prayerleader.com and click on Empowered (under PUBLICATIONS on the right toolbar). There you will find a section on prayer initiatives.

- ☑ Critical: Provide plenty of prayer coverage prior to your event!
- ☑ Coordinate this event with your pastor. His participation and support are critical.
- ☑ Promote your event well in advance. Use posters, bulletin inserts, and announcements from the pulpit. Enter the event on your church calendar if you have one being sure to mark the duration of the initiative.
- ☑ Purchase or prepare prayer initiative materials for every member of your church.
- ☑ If you decide to hold a final prayer rally, plan for music and schedule use of the meeting facility with your church office. Be sure to announce and promote the final rally.

Resources

40 Days of Prayer (Love to Pray) by Al VanderGriend (PrayerShop Publishing) is by far the most complete prayer initiative available. It has a resource kit that provides a teaching DVD, and CDs with promotional material and sermon outlines. Plus it has a valuable booklet on planning your initiative. I also recommend purchasing the *40 Day Strategy and Guidelines* even if you are not doing this prayer initiative. The guidelines booklet has valuable ideas to help you plan any initiative. It is available at www.prayershop.org.

Seek God for the City is an excellent prayer initiative that takes place for the 40 days leading up to Palm Sunday. Information and materials (including materials for children) are available at: www.waymakers.org.

Other excellent prayer initiatives on various topics: *Prayer* *of Jabez* and *Ready for Revival* by Jacquie Tyre can be found at www.praymag.com.

Notes

Women's Prayer Tea

Showcase prayer to the women of your church in a lovely and inviting setting.

Ideally, the Women's Prayer Tea attempts to bring women together through prayer. Creating a lovely and inviting atmosphere where women can connect and be challenged to pray through common struggles is the essence of this event. Bring women together now to foster a structure for sustained prayer in the future.

Essentials

This event can be as elaborate or as simple as you care to make it. Attention to details will be appreciated by participants, but be prepared with lots of helpers if you opt for a more elaborate version of this occasion. A more elaborate event would include enlisting women in advance to "host" a table of six to eight, bringing their china tea sets from home as tableware. In this scenario refreshments would include typical tea fare including finger sandwiches, scones, tea cookies and chocolates (see resources for menu ideas). A simpler version might include a buffet of tea cookies with each woman bringing her own tea cup from home.

Whether you opt for an elaborate or simple version, there are some essential elements that will insure success. Group six to eight women at each table. At each place offer a small gift with a prayer focus—this could be a bookmark prayer guide, an inexpensive blank book to serve as a prayer journal, a magnet with a saying or verse on prayer, etc. Randomly select three seats and affix a sticker to a hidden spot at those place settings. Later during the event the women seated in those chairs will receive a door prize with a prayer focus (consider a book on prayer for women, a more elaborate prayer journal, etc.).

Supply each table with 3 x 5 cards. During the tea, request that each woman fill out her name and any information she cares to share (marital status, family members' names, and specific prayer requests) on the card. The cards will be collected and put into a basket. Before leaving, each woman who filled out a card will select a card at random from the basket. She will then commit to pray for the woman on the card she picked (this can be kept secret and revealed at a later time or you can opt to have them introduce themselves now).

As the women enjoy their tea and refreshments, encourage them to share prayer requests with each other at the table. Allow ample time for them to open up with what is on their hearts before moving into a time of prayer for one another.

The speaker listed on the schedule should be a woman who shares a personal testimony or devotional about prayer that will challenge and encourage. If you cannot find a woman who is able to prepare that kind of presentation, enlist someone to read a story about prayer (see resources for suggestions).

Sample Schedule

P.M.

2:00 – 2:15 Welcome the women and open with prayer.
Explain the schedule of events and encourage the women to share their prayer requests with each other as they enjoy their tea and refreshments. Tell them they will have opportunity to pray for each other later. Point out the prayer gift they have to take home.
Explain the purpose behind the 3 x 5 cards and ask them to fill them out as they chat.
2:15 – 2:45 Tea and Chat
2:45 – 2:50 Collect the 3 x 5 cards in a basket.
2:50 – 3:05 Speaker: Prayer devotional or testimony.
3:05 – 3:35 Pray for one another at each table.
3:35 – 3:45 Pass around the basket of 3 x 5 cards. Each woman who filled out a card should now take one and either keep it secret or introduce herself to the woman for whom she will be praying (pre-determine how you want to handle this).
3:45 – 4:00 Ask women to look for the sticker at their place setting; present door prizes to winners.
Close in prayer and say good-byes.

Don't Forget!

- ☑ Critical: Provide plenty of pre-event prayer coverage!
- ☑ Coordinate date, time and use of meeting space with church office. Make sure your event does not conflict with other events. Trying to hold a Women's Prayer Tea on the weekend of the Women's Scrapbooking Retreat wouldn't work.
- ☑ Promote your event! In addition to bulletin inserts, power point, verbal announcements and inclusion on the church calendar, consider sending individual invitations to this one.
- ☑ The more elaborate the tea, the more helpers you need!
- ☑ Arrange for women to host tables (bring tea service for the number of guests at their table; note: mismatched tea sets are fine and can even add to the charm) or ask each woman to bring her own tea cup.
- ☑ Make sure you have lots of hot water on hand—it goes fast and it takes too long to heat more once you've started your event. Use large electric pots to heat the water and keep it hot, or pre-heat and put in thermal carafes.
- ☑ Make arrangements for refreshments.
- ☑ Prepare for speaker/reader in advance.
- ☑ Secure prayer "favors" for each place setting plus three door prizes.
- ☑ 3 x 5 cards & basket.

Hint: Music by a guest soloist might add a special touch.

Resources

Prayer party favors: bookmark prayer guides on many topics are available at www.prayershop.org.

Door prizes: books on prayer or prayer journals available at www.prayershop.org, subscription to *Pray!*, Keys to the Kingdom prayer-guide key chains at www.prayershop.org. "I prayed for you today" boxed cards by Dayspring would make an excellent gift—available in your Christian bookstore or online at www.dayspring.com.

Articles on prayer (in lieu of a prayer devotional or testimony): Appropriate articles are available in *Pray!*'s online archives at www.praymag.com, but here are two suggestions: "The Power of One" by Brent Haggerty and "A Sister's Prayer and God's Timing" by Tricia McCary Rhodes. Also in the *Discipleship Journal* archives at www.discipleshipjournal.com is "Journey to the Heart of Prayer" by Sandra Higley.

Menu ideas: *If Teacups Could Talk: Sharing a Cup of Kindness with Treasured Friends* by Emilie Barnes (www.amazon.com); also, menus and recipes for high tea offered at http://whatscookingamerica.net/Menu/HighTea.htm.

Notes

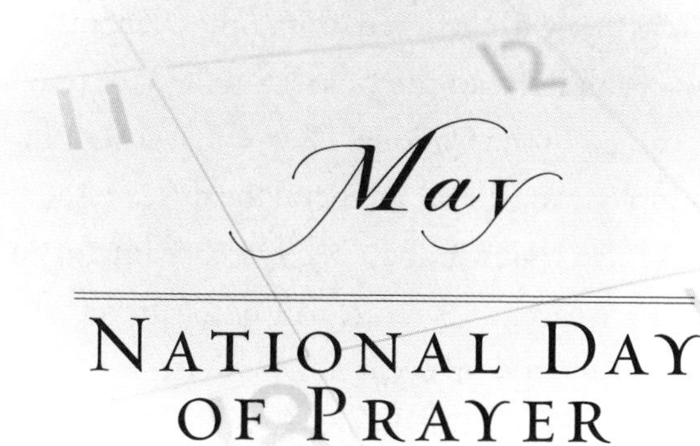

May

National Day of Prayer

Join with pray-ers across the country in prayer for our nation.

The first Thursday of every May marks the observance of the National Day of Prayer. The Continental Congress first called the colonies to prayer in 1775, asking prayer for wisdom as the nation was being formed. President Lincoln continued the call in 1863 with his proclamation of a day of "humiliation, fasting, and prayer." An annual national day of prayer began in 1952 through a joint resolution by Congress, signed by President Truman. The law was then amended in 1988 by President Reagan who permanently set the day as the first Thursday of every May.

The National Day of Prayer Task Force, currently chaired by Shirley Dobson, exists to promote and facilitate this annual observance. Approximately 35,000 registered prayer gatherings are held each year with several million people participating. Your first choice for the National Day of Prayer would be to join with other churches in your area to participate in whatever observances are being held. Not only does this promote unity in the body of Christ as we gather together with believers from other denominations, it also is a show of solidarity to the world as united we pray for our country. You can go to the National Day of Prayer website to find where events in your local area are being held (see resources that follow). You can also choose to be a NDOP coordinator and be in charge of a registered event. If you are new to the prayer movement, you might want to observe an event someone else has planned first before tackling the job of being in charge on your own.

Essentials

Perhaps your area does not hold a registered community event or your church opts to celebrate on its own. If you are planning your own observance, you can choose to hold an all day event or plan an evening-only prayer rally—it's up to you. Included here are sample schedules for an all-day celebration as well as an evening-only prayer rally. Either scenario can be adapted for your situation and used—all or in part—according to your needs.

Remember to take into consideration how much help you have before deciding on your level of participation. These sample schedules can be modified, but here are essential elements for the highlighted segments of the samples.

Church open for prayer: Consider opening your church all or part of the day for participants to drop in to pray. Set up prayer stations around the sanctuary. Provide a beverage bar (coffee, tea, juice, water) for those who are fasting. Create an atmosphere of worship through soft background music on your sound system. You will want one or more people to serve as monitors throughout the event for safety as people come and go.

Prayer Stations: Typically the National Day of Prayer focuses on five major areas: Government, Media, Education, Church and Family. Each prayer station should cover one of these areas with visual prompts and other helps for focused prayer. Prompts can range from physical objects (the American flag for government, a cross for church) to posters or handouts. This is a perfect opportunity to provide prayer guides on the focus areas—see resources for suggestions. Prayer stations should be set up as far apart as possible so that individuals praying at one station do not interrupt prayer at another station. This is especially important if you opt for the evening-only schedule. In that case, you will have more people involved at the prayer stations all at once. Consider setting them up in different areas around the church and leaving you sanctuary open for overflow. Depending on the size of your crowd, you may need to encourage people to make a quick visit to each station to pick up prayer guides and then find a place to sit in meditation and prayer in the sanctuary. Have worship music playing softly in the background.

Prayerwalk: A prayerwalk around the county courthouse or city government buildings can be a featured part of your all-day observance. Other destinations for a prayerwalk might include local schools, television stations or your church in keeping with the five focus areas. See the October Prayerwalking event for how to's.

Children's Focus: NDOP is a great time to get children involved in prayer. Be sure to offer elements in the day that will be of interest to them. During the family picnic, have children write or draw their prayer on a piece of paper that you provide. Tie each prayer to the tail of a helium balloon and release the prayers to heaven simultaneously at the end of the dinner hour. Provide coloring pages for the children to draw their prayers at your prayer stations. Have them sign a "We are praying for you, Mr. President" letter which you later send to the White House along with a group picture. You may opt to hold a separate children's concert of prayer at the same time as the adult version. Or, you might include them in the adult concert but single them out at different points: have all the children come lay hands on the soldiers, for instance, as you pray for the troops and thank God for those willing to lay down their lives for a future of freedom. Include them in as many ways as possible—these are current and future intercessors!

Concert of Prayer: Ending the evening with a concert of prayer covering the major prayer thrusts might be a good finale to the day. Consider finding people in your congregation who symbolize each area of focused prayer to be on hand so that people can gather around them to lay hands on them as they pray. It would be especially appropriate to have a uniformed police officer, fireman, paramedic, and people serving in the armed forces present. If you don't have people serving in the areas who attend your congregation, you might be able to arrange for someone to come visit from those service areas in the city just for the event. See the August Concert of Prayer event for general ideas on this portion of the schedule.

Full Day Sample Schedule

A.M. – P.M.

7:00 a.m. – 3:00 Open your church for people to come and go throughout the day. Provide prayer stations and a beverage bar.

3:00 – 5:00 Organized prayerwalk for critical areas in your city.

5:00 – 6:30 Family picnic on church grounds or potluck in fellowship hall.
Prayer Balloon release.
6:30 – 7:15 Open in prayer and worship. Include patriotic songs and pledge of allegiance. Read call to prayer by the President of the United States or the governor of your state (see resources).
7:15 – 8:30 Concert of Prayer.

Evening Only Sample Schedule

P.M.
5:00 – 6:00 Family picnic on church grounds or potluck in fellowship hall.
Prayer Balloon release.
6:00 – 6:30 Open in prayer and worship. Include patriotic songs and pledge of allegiance. Read call to prayer by the President of the United States or the governor of your state (see resources).
6:30 – 7:30 Invite everyone to spread out to different prayer stations and work their way around until they have prayed at each station. Keep sanctuary open for overflow. Have worship music playing softly in the background.
7:30 – 7:45 Have everyone gather in the sanctuary.
Worship song.
7:45 – 8:25 You have eight minutes for each of the five areas of prayer focus. Ask someone in advance to lead out in prayer for a specified area and then open time for public prayer on that focus. Invite uniformed representatives for each area to stand so that people can lay hands on them or hold their hands out toward them.
8:25 – 8:30 Sing "God Bless America"
Closing prayer.

Don't Forget!

- ☑ Critical: Begin prayer coverage well in advance of your NDOP event!
- ☑ Coordinate date, time and use of meeting space with church office. Plan far enough ahead so that your event takes precedence over other events.
- ☑ Promote your event! The National Day of Prayer Task Force provides bulletin inserts if you care to use them along with other promotional materials such as posters and prayer guides (see resources).
- ☑ You need plenty of helpers—consider assigning each major portion of the day to a helper and their team.
- ☑ Make arrangements for picnic/potluck: preparation, service and clean-up.
- ☑ If using video or audio materials, arrange for needed equipment.
- ☑ Make arrangements for worship and background music.
- ☑ Prepare children's materials in advance: color pages, letter to the President, helium balloons.
- ☑ Decide in advance areas to be prayerwalked. Coordinate transportation to and from the area(s).
- ☑ Arrange for uniformed police officer, fireman, paramedic, members of armed forces to attend.
- ☑ Download copy of proclamation by President or your state governor.
- ☑ Remember that this is a school night and you have

children involved. Be sensitive to end your event at an appropriate time.

Hint: Be sure to plan alternatives for outdoor activities if weather turns bad. For example: your group might be able to pray in the lobby of the city hall if you can't pray outside, but check in advance.

Resources

National Day of Prayer Task Force materials: promotional materials, prayer guides, presidential and gubernatorial proclamations, listing of registered city-wide events, information on becoming an official NDOP coordinator are all available at www.nationaldayofprayer.org

Additional prayer guides for prayer stations available on all NDOP focus areas as well as additional topics at www.prayershop.org.

List of federal government officials: www.nationaldayofprayer.org

List of state government officials: these are usually available at your state government's website. Enter www. followed by the name of your state.gov. (Example: www.colorado.gov or www.georgia.gov).

Notes

June

Men's Prayer Breakfast

Encourage the men of your church to become prayer warriors with a breakfast for champions.

"I want men everywhere to lift up holy hands in prayer."
(1 Timothy 2:8)

Typically women outnumber men when it comes to prayer. It can be difficult to garner the interest of the men in your church toward prayer. The Men's Prayer Breakfast can cast a vision for men that prayer is warfare and requires watchmen, warriors, and champions. It's your mission to introduce them to prayer as the muscle behind what God wants to do in the church. As men are challenged in their thinking and catch a glimpse of their God-given role as members of the "order of Epaphras" (who wrestled in prayer: Eph. 4:12), your prayer team will expand to a more balanced male/female ratio.

Essentials

The draw to this event for most men will be the food and fellowship. While you can have a successful event with a continental breakfast menu, consider offering a heartier breakfast buffet. Perhaps the women in your church will be interested in cooking for this event when they hear that a praying husband might be the result! Another choice is to arrange for your breakfast at a restaurant or hotel that offers private meeting rooms.

Pick a male-oriented prayer theme as part of your promotion. There are many to pick from that would appeal to men: wrestlers, warriors, champions, soldiers, or wall-builders are just a few. Use clip art or photos in keeping with your theme in bulletin inserts or on bulletin boards, etc. Get some traction with a humorous skit or a male announcer outfitted appropriately for your theme (Gladiator garb? Army camis?) marketing the event from the platform. Consider inviting men ages 13 and up. Youth are a seriously under-utilized prayer resource.

As with any prayer event, pre-determine your prayer focus. Is the object to pray for families? To enlist volunteers on the prayer team or man the night watch in your prayer room? Raising the general level of interest in prayer among men is always good, but they are more likely to respond to a clearly defined "mission" if one is offered.

The speaker or presentation at this event is critical. It has to be something that will grab a man's attention and inspire him to step outside his comfort zone. Unlike the Women's Prayer Tea where the relational aspect of "tea and chat" was a central element to the event, the men will probably need entertainment that challenges and motivates. If you don't have a speaker who can pull this off or the ability to bring one in, there are some excellent video alternatives in the resources section that may work for you.

Sample Schedule

Saturday A.M.

7:00 – 7:15 Have coffee bar ready and allow men to fellowship as you wait for latecomers.

7:15 – 7:45 Welcome the men and open with prayer.

Invite men to help themselves to the buffet. Make sure that they feel welcome to refill their plates even after the presentation has started.

7:45 Introduce speaker or video.

7:45 – 9:00? Presentation (if a longer video is used feel free to start it earlier as the men begin eating).

9:00 If the object of your event is to enlist the men to participate on a prayer team or in a prayer room, etc., now is the time to pass around sign-up sheets.

9:00 – 9:30 Open a time of prayer for men to pray asking God to give them a passion to become prayer warriors (keep using your theme throughout the event).

Close in prayer and dismiss.

Don't Forget!

- ☑ Pre-event prayer coverage is a must!
- ☑ Coordinate date, time and use of meeting space with church office. Make sure your event does not conflict with other events. Trying to hold a Men's Prayer Breakfast

on the weekend of the Father/Son Camp Out would not be wise.

- ☑ Promote your event! In addition to bulletin inserts, and inclusion on the church calendar, personal promotion (men inviting men personally) and humorous announcements will attract attention and encourage participation.
- ☑ Make arrangements for food: preparation, service and clean-up.
- ☑ Prepare for speaker/video in advance. If using a video, arrange for needed equipment.
- ☑ Prepare sign up sheets if needed attached to 3 or 4 clipboards to circulate (attach a pen or pencil to the clipboard).
- ☑ Give everyone who wants to participate an opportunity to pray, but ask a few in advance to be prepared to pray on the focused topic.

Hint: If finances are an issue, an all-you-can-eat pancake breakfast might be a good choice.

Resources

If your budget allows, consider presenting each participant with a book about men waging war through prayer. It will sustain the encouragement to get involved. *Fight on Your Knees* is available at a discount at www.praymag.com.

Alternatives to speaker: The Sentinel Group offers several excellent motivational videos/DVDs. *Transformation I, Transformation II, Let the Seas Resound,* and *An Unconventional War* are available at www.sentinelgroup.com.

Notes

Notes

July

Prayer for the Nations Rally

Reach out and touch the world through this global-focused event.

"Ask of me, and I will make the nations your inheritance, the ends of the earth your possession." (Ps. 2:8)

Through a Prayer for the Nations Rally, you are providing your participants a passport to view the needs and desperation of a hurting world. You are expanding your congregation's horizons, allowing it to participate in the Great Commission through prayer. If your people seem stuck in a rut, only wanting to pray about their own immediate, everyday needs, a Prayer for the Nations Rally could be just what you are looking for to pull them out of their small narrowly focused lives into the bigger picture.

Essentials

Again, this event can be as simple or as detailed as you care to make it, but at the very least, it requires a lot of homework prior to the rally. The more information and visual prayer prompts you can provide, the better your group will be able to connect with the prayer targets.

You'll want to highlight several foreign countries for the evening. Decide in advance which countries are of primary interest to your group. Perhaps your church supports missionaries in several countries, or your youth group regularly visits a certain country on short term mission's trips. Maybe someone's son or daughter is serving in Iraq or Afghanistan and you regularly pray for him or her—that would make those countries an ideal choice. You might want to feature countries where the Christians are most persecuted such as the Sudan or Indonesia. Or maybe your heart is to cover unreached people groups. There are lots of options, but your event will be more meaningful if you give some thought to the specific areas targeted.

Enlist helpers to be in charge of the various countries you are highlighting. This will lighten your load and it is always easier to boost attendance when others have a vested interest in the event. Depending on space available, have each helper design a prayer station or table representing their country. This can be as simple as some wall space with maps, photos, and bulleted information. A more elaborate version might have a booth for each country with brochures, handmade items, props representing that nation's exports, and your helpers dressed in native garb. Whatever you do, make the material appealing and interesting to get your attendees connected.

If you decide to serve food at this event, you can go all the way with an international potluck featuring foods from the countries being highlighted. Or, go simple with light snacks at each booth (chips and salsa for Mexico or mini-egg rolls for China, etc.). Set up a separate beverage station where your participants can get coffee, tea, etc. The sample schedule in this chapter assumes you are offering light snacks only, so adjust your time schedule accordingly if you intend to start with lunch or dinner. If you are holding this event in July, consider holding it outdoors, but be sure to have a backup plan if the weather doesn't cooperate.

As each guest arrives, hand them a program explaining the evening's focus. Before the event, write the name of one of the featured countries on the top of each program (if you have five countries and 50 attendees, each of the five countries will have 10 prayer partners for the event). This will assure that each country is adequately covered in prayer. While everyone will circulate to view information at all the stations, participants will want to spend the most time at the booth representing their assigned country to learn as much as possible before the prayer time begins.

Each of your helpers will need to research the country they are hosting and prepare prayer points for the pray-ers who have been assigned to pray for that nation. These prayer guides should include significant economical hardships, persecution, information on government and national religion, and the percentage of Christians in the population if possible. The more information, the better equipped your participants will be to pray. See resources at the end of this chapter for places to find this kind of information.

If you can, enlist help from someone willing to lead a children's group to pray for the nations. While the adults spend time praying for their assigned group, let the children participate in their own lively version. For ideas on how to plan children's prayer activities, see the Kid's Prayer Fest in the chapter on Alternative Events.

Sample Schedule

Saturday or Sunday P.M.

6:00 – 7:00 Have coffee/beverage bar ready. As each attendee arrives, hand them a brochure with the name of their assigned country written at the top. Encourage them to circulate and look at all the stations but to pay particular attention to their assigned country. Allow attendees to fellowship and enjoy the international snack foods.
7:00 – 7:20 Welcome everyone and ask them to sit in groups by assigned countries. Have your helpers hand out prayer points to the people assigned to the country for which they are responsible.
Begin with prayer asking the Holy Spirit to open your eyes to the needs of the nations. Ask that your hearts be connected to God's heart regarding each lost soul represented.
Worship (include songs that focus on the lost and the nations).
7:20 – 8:20 Allow each group to pray for their assigned country assisted by the prayer points provided.
8:20 – 8:30 Worship.
Closing prayer.

Hint: Consider expanding your time to include a testimony and encouragement to pray from a visiting missionary.

Don't Forget!

- ☑ Critical: Provide plenty of prayer coverage well in advance of your event!
- ☑ Coordinate date, time and use of meeting space with church office. Make sure your event does not conflict with other events.
- ☑ Promote your event! Use bulletin inserts, power point and verbal announcements, posters and inclusion on the church calendar.
- ☑ Make arrangements for coffee/beverage bar: preparation, service and clean-up.
- ☑ Make arrangements for music.
- ☑ Enlist helpers to prepare prayer stations/booths. Make sure they understand what is required of them (snacks, visual prompts, prayer points, etc.). Encourage them to make this as inviting and interesting as possible. Offer to help them by pointing them toward the resources they need. A week before your event, contact each one to see how they are doing and what features their station or booth will include.
- ☑ Prepare programs in advance describing the event focus. Assign countries by writing the name of a different highlighted country on the top of each program. Try to keep your prayer groups covering the different countries evenly distributed.

Resources

Operation World: *Operation World* CD-ROM contains the full (English language) text, as well as all maps, charts, and tables from the *Operation World* book by Patrick Johnstone and Jason Mandryk (published in September 2001, by Paternoster Publishing). In addition, the CD contains the full *Operation World* research database, along with additional research resources for every country. Available at www.prayershop.org.

Unreached People Group Profiles: Each profile contains a photo, map, and information about the lifestyles, customs, and beliefs of the people. More importantly, it lists spiritual strongholds and addresses specific prayer needs. Available at www.global12project.com.

Prayer Maps: Every Home for Christ offers the latest information for every nation including heads of state, population, percentage of Christians, and restrictions on evangelical efforts. Available at www.ehc.org.

Notes

Notes

August

Concert of Prayer

Orchestrate a symphony of harmonic prayer to an audience of One!

". . . they lifted up their voice to God with one accord . . ." (Acts 4:24, NLT).

An organized concert of prayer will give your congregation context for powerful and enjoyable corporate prayer. In this framework, your people will begin to see possibilities that extend beyond a traditional prayer meeting where one person at a time prays aloud while everyone else fights the urge to doze off. A concert of prayer keeps things focused, lively and in sync. If your group has never done so, they will be surprised and pleased that they are able to spend an extended time in focused prayer. It is a difficult task to get people to pray on the same topic—and stay there—until the Holy Spirit guides to a different area. A concert of prayer begins to train them in that "one accord" mindset with everyone praying about one topic for a short period before moving to a new focus.

A concert of prayer works well as a stand-alone event, but is also a nice addition at the beginning or end of a seminar or conference. It is often used to round out other National Day of Prayer activities.

Essentials

A concert of prayer is probably one of the easier events to plan. The most critical element is to decide your focus or topic. We have provided you with a general concert format that will always work well. However, you may want to customize it by reworking the topics in keeping with something specific your church is praying toward.

You will need a concert "conductor." You or someone else will act as emcee for the evening, directing each change of focus. Keep your instructions brief and simple but make sure that everyone knows what is expected of them at all times. The evening is broken up into 10 minute segments. As with any of the events in this book, feel free to manipulate the schedule to suit your needs. Shorten/lengthen or eliminate/add segments as desired. Remember, it isn't a precise format that is important. You are simply providing an opportunity for your people to connect with and be ministered to by the Holy Spirit.

The best setting for a concert of prayer is the sanctuary or a large room with chairs that can be moved into several circles of 6 to 8. Make enough circles to accommodate your total number of attendees. If your people are used to looking at an overhead screen for worship songs, you may want to include words to a few songs on the handouts. Not everyone will be facing forward so it will be difficult for some to see the screen. Encourage everyone to bring a Bible, notebook and pen, and to wear comfortable clothes.

Prepare a handout for each place that includes the schedule for the concert to orient everyone to the order of service. For the sample concert below, you will need to handwrite the name of one of our government officials on the program. Put a different name on each handout so that as many of our country's officials are covered individually in prayer as possible. If you have a small group you may want to list more than one name. At one point you will be asking people to read aloud from their favorite praise passage in the Bible. On your handout, list some praise references for someone to use if they are drawing a blank and can't think of a passage on their own. Also, it would be nice to have one praise passage typed out on the reverse side of the handout for anyone who forgot to bring their Bible.

Refreshments are definitely not necessary at this event although it would be advisable to serve coffee, tea and water or other beverages.

Sample Schedule

P.M.

7:00 – 7:10 Have coffee/beverage bar ready. Allow attendees to fellowship as you wait for latecomers and everyone finds a seat.

7:10 – 7:20 Welcome everyone and open with prayer.

Explain format.

Worship song.

Focus Area: Heart Preparation

7:20 - 7:30 Conductor reads aloud: Ps. 100:3-5.

Corporate: Open a time for corporate praise. Together as a large group, have individuals stand and praise God for *all that He is.*

7:30 – 7:40 Conductor reads aloud: Ps. 66:18; 1 John 1:8-9.
Individuals: Take first five minutes for quiet personal reflection and personal confession.
Corporate: Worship song.
7:40 – 7:50 Conductor leads out in prayer of thanksgiving for work of the Cross and forgiveness of sins and privilege of prayer.
Circle groups: Invite circle groups to spend time thanking God for all the *things He does for us.*

Focus Area: Local Church Intercession
7:50 – 8:00 Conductor reads Eph. 6:18-20 and invites everyone to pair up within their circle groups to pray for each other's needs.
8:00 – 8:10 Circle Groups: Stand and hold hands.
Pray for spiritual renewal and revival on a personal, local church, and worldwide church basis.
8:10 – 8:20 Corporate: large group joins in prayer for pastoral staff needs. Have people feel free to move to a pastoral staff member or elder, etc. closest to them to lay hands on them as they pray.

Focus Area: Outreach
8:20 – 8:30 Conductor reads: Jn. 4:34-36.
Circle groups: Take five minutes to pray for lost we know personally.
Large group: Take five minutes to pray for lost around the world and missionaries. Pray for individual countries as led.
8:30 – 8:40 Conductor reads: 1 Tim. 2:1-3.
Individuals: Take 5 minutes to pray silently for the government leader(s) listed on their personal handout.
Circle groups: Take 5 minutes to pray for our country/troops.

Finale of Praise

8:40 – 9:00 Worship song(s)

Corporate: Invite everyone to make a joyful noise! Everyone reads simultaneously their favorite praise passage from the Bible out loud (with gusto!). (On the handout provide some appropriate passages if someone is drawing a blank—see resources for ideas).

Conductor: invites everyone to give God a standing ovation.

Closing prayer.

Hint: Play praise music softly in the background for a nice touch throughout the concert.

Don't Forget!

- ☑ Critical: Your event needs plenty of prayer coverage ahead of time!
- ☑ Coordinate date, time and use of meeting space with church office. Make sure your event does not conflict with other events.
- ☑ Promote your event! Use bulletin inserts, power point and verbal announcements, posters and inclusion on the church calendar.
- ☑ Make arrangements for coffee/beverage bar: preparation, service and clean-up.
- ☑ Make arrangements for music.
- ☑ Prepare handouts in advance with schedule of events, words to worship songs used, name(s) of government officials, praise references and typed out praise passage for finale.
- ☑ Set up chairs in circles of 6 to 8.

Resources

Praise references to include on hand out: Include references on the handout for the praise finale in case someone needs suggestions. Here are a few: Ex. 18:9-11; Ps. 86:6-15, 103, 104, 115, 117, 148, 150; Lk. 1:47-55, 68-79; Rev. 19:1-10.

List of government officials: a list of your state government officials can usually be found at www. plus the name of your state .gov (example: www.texas.gov or www.california.gov). Federal government officials are available at www.nationaldayofprayer.org.

Books that will help: *Fresh Encounters* by Daniel Henderson (NavPress) includes several concert of prayer formats. *And the Place Was Shaken* by John Franklin (Broadman & Holman) is a book on leading dynamic prayer meetings. Both books are available at www.prayershop.org.

Notes

Notes

Alternative Events

For one reason or another, you may find that one or two of the events previously highlighted would not be a good fit for your church. Three additional events are offered here as alternatives:

- Kid's Prayer Fest
- Prayer Journey
- Pastoral Staff Prayer Saturation event.

Plus, we have added a "Plan Your Own Event" section, which will help you facilitate an event you come up with.

Alternative #1 Kid's Prayer Fest

Helping children learn to pray is truly a joy. Not only are you leaving a heritage with the future generation of intercessors and prayer leaders, you are empowering them as a powerful prayer force in their own right. Jesus told us that we have to become like little children with their faith and ability to trust before we can enter the kingdom

(Mt. 18:3). In the Psalms we are told that the praise of infants and children is powerful spiritual warfare against the enemy (Ps. 8:2). We need their prayers NOW, not later.

Essentials

These are children, so keep it focused, flexible and fun!

Make sure they understand the issues surrounding the prayer **focus** you've chosen. Any pictures or visuals you can use—especially pictures of children who are touched by the situation—will help their hearts connect. If you are praying for a war-torn country, pictures of children saying good-bye to their soldier parents as well as children affected by war in the country itself are good visuals to use. If you are praying for a country that experiences starvation and persecution, try to include photos with children. Be sensitive. Don't show anything that is too graphic in nature, but let them connect with the faces and surroundings. Remember that most of them have not been to a third-world country and most of them do not watch the news on TV, so they need something to help them make the jump from their situation to someone who is hurting in an entirely different context.

Be **flexible**! The Bible is full of things that were done symbolically to create change in the status quo. The use of salt (Jdg. 9:44-46, 2 Ki. 2:19-21), a piece of wood (Ex. 14:22-25), arrows (2 Ki. 13:17-19), drawings and ropes (Ezk. 4:1-6) are only a few. Let the children "stomp" on the enemy (Lk. 10:19), make a joyful noise (Ps. 98:4), or walk seven times around a symbolic stronghold before shouting, "Victory is the Lord's!" (Josh. 3:6-5). Children love to touch things with their hands—consider providing a poster-sized picture of your prayer target (the President, for instance) for them to lay hands on as they pray. Children are GREAT prayerwalkers. Take them on a group walk around the neighborhood with a game of "I Spy" to find clues to help them pray along the way.

Be sure to provide **fun**, creative ways for the children to pray. Remember, you are trying to get them to connect with God—and He created fun! He is not interested in impressive words and phrases. He told adults to become like little children, so don't inhibit—instead release them to enjoy prayer. See the Resources section on where to find more help with children, but here are just a few ideas of ways to make prayer fun:

- **Picture prayers.** Let children draw their prayers for the subject at hand. Leader should highlight different prayer points for the children on the focused area as they draw their requests. You could even put up butcher paper on a large wall and let them create a mural with their prayers on a certain theme.
- **Global prayers.** Get an inflatable globe (available at educational toy stores and a variety of online retailers) and allow the children to form a circle and toss it to one another. Whoever catches it prays for someone in the nation closest to their right thumb (be prepared to help them figure out which country it is).
- **Blind-fold prayers.** Put a large map of the world on the wall and blind-fold the children one at a time. Let them walk forward and tag a country as a prayer target with praying hands cut from construction paper (similar to "pin-the-tail-on-the-donkey"). Once they "tag" a country (Japan, for instance), all the children declare in unison in their loudest voices: "Jesus is Lord over Japan!"
- **Musical chairs.** Set up enough chairs for the children minus one. Let each child hold a small flag of a different nation (if you can't find actual mini-flags, make paper flags or simply the name of a

country printed on construction paper). Play music and allow the children to circle around the chairs. Stop the music intermittently. When the music stops, the children take a seat. The child who ended up without a seat has the center of attention as they lead all the children to pray for the nation whose flag he or she holds.

- **Just like me.** Let each child take a turn praying for children with whom they can identify personally. Example: an eight-year-old boy might pray for all the boys in Africa who were born on his birthday or all the boys in the world with red hair, etc.
- **Popcorn prayers.** Have the children sit in a circle and take turns as they pop up with a one sentence prayer about the topic. The next person is ready to pop up the minute the first one is finished.

Schedule

Part of being flexible is to stay loose and let the Holy Spirit guide. Choose a few fun activities and see where it takes you. Children aren't nearly as concerned with schedules and agendas as adults. An hour and a half is probably the maximum amount of time you want to allow, including time for refreshments and kids' worship songs.

Don't Forget!

☑ Cover your prayer event well in advance—enlist adults to pray for the event while it is taking place. Grandparents are a great source of intercessors for this type of event!

☑ Coordinate date, time and use of meeting space with church office. Make sure your event does not conflict with other events.

- ☑ Promote your event! Use bulletin inserts, power point and verbal announcements, posters and inclusion on the church calendar. You will want to promote this to the children's groups as well as their parents.
- ☑ Make arrangements for snacks and beverages: preparation, service and clean-up.
- ☑ After choosing your activities, make sure you have all supplies needed on hand: paper, pencils or crayons, inflatable globe, visual prayer prompts, maps, blind-folds, etc.

Resources

Some important websites with resources on teaching kids to pray: www.praykids.com: *Pray*Kids! magazine and leaders guides. www.kidsinministry.com: Books, CDs, conference materials on prayer for children.

Books

Growing Up Prayerful, edited by Jon Graf, et al. (www.navpress.com)

Let the Children Pray by Esther Ilnisky (www.childreninministry.com)

When Children Pray by Cheri Fuller (www.prayershop.org)

Curriculum

KidsGap: Teaching Children to be Kingdom Intercessors by Jenny Almquist (www.prayershop.org)

*Pray*Kids! (www.praymag or www.prayershop.org)

Other Materials

"Children's World Prayer Map" (www.ehc.org)
Prayer coloring books and *P.R.A.Y.* curriculum (www.nationaldayofprayer.org)
Prayer guides: T.H.U.M.B. cards and other children's prayer guides available at www.prayershop.org.

Alternative #2 Prayer Journey

If you are blessed to be able to take your group on a prayer journey to another country, it will probably be life-changing. The impact of seeing the needs and desperation of people first hand will supply a lasting impression to help your group connect in prayer with a heart for the lost. There's something about actually looking into the faces, experiencing the conditions, and feeling the spiritual oppression that seems to hang in the air of a third-world country that fuels intercession like nothing else. The benefits are multiple: not only are you bringing the Holy Spirit into the area and advancing the kingdom through prayer, you are also equipping your group with a point-of-reference resource that will last a life-time.

Prayer journeys, for the most part, are handled in a similar fashion as a prayerwalk. Refer to the chapter on prayerwalking for details not listed here. In this case, three options are being listed so as to accommodate all situations: a prayer journey to a foreign land, a local prayer journey, and a virtual prayer journey.

Essentials

Any prayer journey (foreign, local or virtual) requires preparation. You can turn any vacation you might be taking into an instant prayer journey by allowing the people and things you observe around you to prompt your prayers. But to get the most out of a trip made for the specific purpose of prayer, you and your team will want to spend an extraordinary amount of time asking God to reveal His plan and purpose.

Every member of your team should be assigned to do research into the history and culture of the area to which you will be traveling. You'll be able to gather helpful information from a wide variety of sources, secular and religious. Even articles in the encyclopedia about the artwork of a country can yield information to fuel your prayers. For instance, every handcrafted item in Bali is dedicated to use in the Hindu temples. When artists in Java create a portrait, they pray for spirits to enter the piece as they are painting the eyes. These are important clues as you try to create a "spiritual map" of the area you are visiting. Ask the Holy Spirit for discernment as you read up on customs, superstitions, religion and economic and political factors that govern an area.

You can benefit from information gathered from previous prayer journeys made to a specific area, but do not rely on that entirely. God has a specific purpose for sending you and your group to this area at this time and may want you to deal with entirely different issues than former journeyers. Your unique mix of life experiences and spiritual gifts along with the changes that have occurred in the area will set your prayer journey apart.

You will want to select a time for your departure far enough in advance to allow for the preparation already mentioned, but also for fundraising and to allow your participants to get time off of work, etc. Summer is usually a good time to try something like this since many people have vacations, school is out, etc. However, don't forget to take into consideration the weather conditions of the area you will be visiting. What might be nice prayerwalking weather at this time of year in our country could be frigid conditions there, so plan accordingly.

A critical part of planning for any foreign or local prayer journey is to acquire a team of intercessors who will stay behind and provide a prayer shield for your group as you travel. This team needs to be apprised of your schedule and given specific prayer requests as frequently as possible. In this age of e-mail there is more of an ability to keep regular prayer requests coming to your prayer team back home than ever before. Be sure to utilize this valuable tool.

Foreign

Obviously, a foreign prayer journey will require a great deal more of everything: time, money and groundwork. In addition to spiritual mapping of the area, you will have to make travel preparations including passports, immunizations, transportation, hotels, etc. Dealing with a travel agency that specializes in prayer journeys will be an enormous help to you because they understand your purpose. Travel agencies do not usually announce that they help send prayer journeyers to foreign countries due to security issues, so you may have to ask around until you find a Christian travel agent who would understand the sensitivity of what you want to accomplish.

Local

A local prayer target is a great way to get your feet wet when it comes to prayer journeys. "Local" refers to any area within the continental United States. You may opt to take a trip to Washington D.C., your state capitol, or your county courthouse. Maybe there is a "high place" in your region—an area of concentrated spiritual activity of the enemy that draws your attention.

Anything outside of your city will require some of the same considerations you would make in a foreign scenario, specifically transportation and hotels if you plan a multiple day event. But you won't need to deal with language barriers or issues such as currency, passports and immunizations.

Virtual

Planning a virtual prayer journey is the next best thing to being there. Clearly, you will miss the benefits of the sights, sounds, smells and feel of an on-site journey, but having your group take time to discern the spiritual needs of an area while you provide sensory touch points to help them connect with the culture will heighten their ability to connect in prayer. To get a feel for the kind of preparation you would need to do to achieve "virtual" status, refer to the July Prayer for the Nations Rally. Select a city, region or country and reproduce it to the best of your ability using maps, posters, photographs, videos, artifacts and even ethnic foods from the area. Have a missionary share slides of the people and conditions; check your local library and travel agent for resources, brochures, videos, etc. Don't forget to utilize the internet—it's a valuable tool when trying to compile the elements for your virtual trip.

Schedule

A schedule for your prayer journey will need to be devised based on your destination. Remember to give ample time at each stop; don't exhaust your participants with an over-zealous schedule. Foreign prayer journeys will need to take jet lag into account. If your local prayer journey is in your immediate area, the schedule for a prayerwalk may work for you, so refer to that chapter. In all cases, briefing and debriefing sessions are helpful. You will probably want to do that daily on a multiple day event.

Don't Forget!

- ☑ Spending adequate time in prayer in advance is the only way your prayer journey will be successful in the spiritual realm. Secure intercessors to cover your time away on a local or foreign prayer journey as well.
- ☑ Coordinate date, time and use of meeting space for a virtual prayer journey with church office. Make sure your virtual event does not conflict with other major church events. Foreign and local journeys need to be coordinated with your church administrative team; however, it will not be as critical if they conflict with other church events since only a small group will be going.
- ☑ Promote your event! Use bulletin inserts, power point and verbal announcements, posters and inclusion on the church calendar. If fundraising is needed, you will want to begin promoting this months in advance.
- ☑ Do your groundwork—make travel and hotel arrange-

ments, investigate information on passports, immunizations, weather, etc. The more information the better!
- ☑ Have all of your participants involved in discerning the spiritual needs of the area in question by studying history, culture, religion, etc.

Resources

Operation World: *Operation World* CD-ROM contains research resources for every country. Available at www.prayershop.org.

Spiritual mapping information: The Sentinel Group www.sentinelgroup.org. Eddie & Alice Smith of U.S. Prayer Center www.prayerbookstore.com.

Prayer Guides: *Praying with Passion: Life-Changing Prayers for Those who Walk in Darkness* by Tommi Femrite. www.win1040.com.

Books for Further Reading

Authority to Tread by Becca Greenwood is available at www.christianharvestintl.org.

WindoWatchman II, encouraging testimonies of prayer journeyers to the 10/40 Window is available at www.win1040.com.

Alternative #3 Pastoral Staff Prayer-Saturation Event

If held during Clergy Appreciation Month (October), this event would be an ideal way to bless your shepherds. Similar to a prayer initiative, this event enlists the entire congregation to participate in a month of focused, united prayer coverage for your pastoral staff.

If you are launching a new prayer focus in your church, or trying to bring life into a prayer ministry that has never gotten off the ground, this could be a great way to get going. Not only does it signal your intent to come alongside your church leadership team as support for them, it also is a great point to begin an ongoing pastoral prayer shield.

After participating in this event, some of your congregation will decide that this is something they would like to become part of on a continual basis. Its appeal for many will be that the praying they do takes place in their own home when it is convenient for their schedule.

Essentials

You'll want to make sure that each member of your pastoral staff is covered adequately in prayer. During event promotions and throughout the month, make it clear that everyone is invited to pray for as many of the leadership team as they want, but that they will be assigned to cover a particular pastoral staff member as their primary target. Remember to include people who are serving in a volunteer position who might otherwise be paid in a larger church: a worship leader/pastor or a Sunday school superintendent might be examples.

Take your church directory and divide the number of family and single-person units evenly among the number of people on your pastoral staff. For instance, if you have five people on staff, and have 100 family/single-person units in the congregation, each of the five in leadership will have at least 20 praying for them.

Your pastoral team will not look kindly on this prayer thrust if they have to answer excessive emails or telephone calls from well-meaning pray-ers asking for requests. Ahead of time, ask each member of the pastoral staff to submit prayer requests in the four following categories: ministry, family, spiritual/physical and vision/goals. Give those requests to the assigned family/single-person units, reminding them not to contact the pastor directly overwhelming them with extra work (unless he invites them to do so). Each week you will be reminding your pray-ers to cover their assigned pastor in prayer especially in the area of focus for that week. Depending on the size of your congregation, you can do this by mail, phone or as an insert in the bulletin.

When you connect with each family/single-person unit to give them their assigned pastoral staff member for prayer coverage, encourage them to send at least one card during the month to that pastor to let him/her know they are praying. You might want to provide "I'm praying for you" cards for this purpose to help them follow through.

At the end of the month you may want to provide sign-up opportunities for those who would like to continue to provide prayer coverage for the ministers in your congregation.

Schedule

Feel free to spread these different prayer topics out—a different one each week as our sample shows—or combine these areas into guides that cover all the topics each week.

• **Week One:** Ministry Needs
Pray for their particular area of ministry in the church.
• **Week Two:** Family Needs
Pray for their family members and individual needs they might have as well as healthy family relationships.

• **Week Three:** Spiritual/Physical Needs
Pray for their spiritual and physical needs including time in the Word and prayer, a deeper walk with the Lord and physical needs (financial, health, etc.).

• **Week Four:** Vision/Goals
Pray for the things they hope to see accomplished in their area of ministry, long-term as well as short-term.

Don't Forget!

☑ As always, pre-event prayer coverage is an absolute.

☑ Promote your event! Use bulletin inserts, power point and verbal announcements, posters and inclusion on the church calendar.

☑ Divide the members of your pastoral staff and assign them to specific family/single-person units for prayer. Make sure coverage is equal. Let each family/single person unit know who they are praying for during the month.

☑ Encourage (perhaps provide) cards to be sent to the pastoral team member letting him or her know he or she is being prayed for.

☑ Each week, remind pray-ers of the prayer focus for that week.

☑ Optional: provide sign-up opportunities for those who would like to continue to provide a prayer shield for church leadership.

Resources

Prayer guides: It might be helpful to provide prayer guides for your congregation to give them direction in prayer. Excellent prayer guides directed toward praying for your pastor, church, financial needs, health issues, children, etc. are available at www.prayershop.org.

Books for Further Reading

Preyed on or Prayed For by Terry Teykl
Prayer Shield by Peter Wagner
Partners in Prayer by John Maxwell
All books are available at www.prayershop.org.

Notes

How to Plan Your Own Event

Going through this book may have started the wheels turning in your head. Already you are beginning to think through specialized prayer events that could be tailored for your church. The possibilities are endless and simply a matter of pre-planning and combining elements of other events that work well for your situation.

As you plan, here are some questions to ask yourself as you try to come up with creative events that will fit your unique circumstances:

- **Who is your target audience?** Who are you trying to reach through the event you want to plan? Think through specifics: gender, age-group, and life-circumstance. For instance, you might want to plan something for stay-at-home moms with pre-school aged children. Or maybe teens are the ones you want to reach. The more specific you can be, the better.
- **What is your purpose?** This involves more than just your desire to get more people praying. Are you trying to provide prayer

coverage for a certain group or event? What is your prayer focus: global evangelism, hiring a new pastor, spiritual renewal for your congregation? Are you hoping to introduce them to a new "type" of prayer they may not be used to (such as contemplative prayer or corporate, kingdom-focused prayer)? Is this a one-time event, or are you hoping to repeat it periodically (weekly, monthly, quarterly)?

- **What other considerations factor into the mix?** What time of year are you planning the event? That might determine whether you plan an indoor or outdoor event. What is the size of your group? That will make a difference on where you plan to meet. What budget do you have for this event? This will limit or increase your options. Keep local geography and surrounding features in mind as you plan. They might just be the perfect backdrop for what you want to achieve.

The End Result. Remember, with every event your goal is to provide an inviting opportunity for people to connect with the heart of God in a prayer experience that will accomplish bringing His kingdom on earth, just as it is in heaven. Keep your structure loose and flexible so that it can be changed if the Holy Spirit leads you in a different way. It is possible to structure the Holy Spirit right out of the picture. "Okay, you have exactly six minutes to come forward and have someone pray over you" is probably not going to garner the connection with God that you are hoping to achieve.

Think Outside the Box. Don't be afraid to try something different. Even the smallest change can freshen up a stale venue. If you always hold your Wednesday night prayer meeting in the sanctuary, sitting in the pews, consider sitting in the choir loft looking out over the auditorium. This new "view" may open all kinds of doors for praying for your pastor, the worship team, and the people listening. If the weather is nice, hold your prayer meeting outdoors or at a nearby park—or turn it into an impromptu prayerwalk around the church property.

The Basics. Every event will require preparation, prayer coverage and promotion. But there are other elements that can make it or break it. If your event must include food of any kind, be sure you plan for more than enough help to set up, serve, and tear down. Keep it easy. You don't want all your intercessors in the kitchen washing dishes all night—that would defeat your purpose.

Music is a prime consideration. If you are blessed to have a worship team at your church, begin cultivating a relationship with them to further prayer in your church. After all, worship IS prayer. The right music creates an atmosphere that makes it easier to get in the flow of prayer. There's something about it that helps you stay focused and in the zone. If you don't have a worship team, you might find a single guitar player who would like to work with you. Even your church pianist might be willing to provide soft background music as you pray—provided, of course, you have a piano where you are meeting. If all else fails, get a boom box and someone who learns to be proficient at fading in and out with appropriate worship CDs.

Your sound system is another critical feature. If you have a large group and people in the back can't hear, that's a problem--so plan accordingly.

Putting It All Together. Once you've thought through your target audience, your purpose, your budget, your locale, etc., you can creatively provide a platform for prayer that will encourage participation. If you live near hiking trails, and your target is the teens in your church, take them on a sunrise prayer hike. Or how about sunrise prayer for your city from a "high place" nearby? If you live near a lake and have access to a boat (or can rent one)—push out from the shore to pray! You may inspire them to a prayer life like Jesus had.

Once you break down the "who, what, when, where and how," ask your Creator God to help you think creatively. He'll help you iron out the details so that your prayer event is everything it can be. He is on your side. He wants to see prayer flourish in your church. And remember, always keep the main thing, the main thing—never let the features of your event crowd out its ultimate purpose: prayer.

Appendix A

Speakers' List

There are many excellent teachers/motivators whose life work centers around assisting the local church in building its prayer focus. Here is a partial, alphabetical list of speakers who would do an excellent job if you plan to hold an equipping seminar in your church:

Bergel, Gary P.
President, Intercessors for America/Youth Interceding for America
PO Box 915
Purcellville, VA 20134
(540) 751-0980
ifa@ifapray.org; garybergel@aol.com
Areas of expertise: *Motivation, corporate intercession and fasting, prayer as lifestyle, solitude. Draws illustrations from prayer lives of Abraham, Jesus of Nazareth, early church.*
Special considerations: *Enjoys multi-ethnic, multi-generational, and youth groups ages 10-35.*
Preview CD available on request.

Conner, Dennis & Betty Jo
Prayer Coaches, Called to Serve
PO Box 850905
Richardson, Texas 75085
(888) 772-9446
calledtoserve@tx.rr.com
Website: www.cts@bahop.org
Areas of expertise: *Motivation & training in building a house of prayer, prayer seminars/workshops (various topics), prayer-focused retreats.*
Special considerations: *Require travel, lodging, meals plus honorarium or love offering.*
Preview audio tape available on request.

Femrite, Tommi
GateKeepers International
15245 Jessie Drive
Colorado Springs, CO 80921
(719) 488-8148; (719) 488-8332 (fax)
info@gatekeepersintl.org
Areas of expertise: *Helps identify, train, equip and empower spiritual gatekeepers in churches, etc.*
Special considerations: *Transportation, food and lodging must be covered along with food and lodging for her intercessor.*

Graddy, Jim
Harvest Prayer Ministries
7246 E. St. Rd. 44 Lot 8W
Wildwood, FL 34785
(352) 330-6216
jim@harvestprayer.com

Areas of expertise: *Facilitator for Learning to Love to Pray seminar; motivation; prayer basics; development of local prayer ministries.*
Special considerations: *Prefer southeast region but available for any area.*
Preview audio tape available on request.

Graf, Jon
President, Church Prayer Leaders Network
Vice-President, Harvest Prayer Ministries
11969 E. Davis Ave.
Brazil, IN 47834
(812) 446-9091
jong@harvestprayer.com
Areas of expertise: *Especially gifted at encouraging the average pew sitter to desire more to grow in prayer. Also good at challenging church leadership.*
Special Considerations: *Requires honorarium, all travel and hotel expenses be covered, and that he can sell books at event.*
Preview audio tape available on request.

Lemmons, Dr. Albert G.
Prayer Matters
2047 Baxter Lane
Franklin, TN 37069
(615) 599-6091
prayermatters@juno.com
Areas of expertise: *Offers seminars on prayer enrichment, spiritual warfare, the prayer life and faith of George Muller, and the ministry of intercession.*
Preview CDs available on request.

Miglioratti, Phil

Facilitator, National Pastors' Prayer Network
1130 Randville Dr. 1D
Palatine, IL 60074
(847) 991-0153
phil@nppn.org

Areas of expertise: *Facilitates corporate prayer, seminars on prayer basics and corporate prayer dynamics. Also gifted in the area of city reaching.*

Preview audio tape available at www.nppn.org.

Noel, Jeff

Vice President of Teaching, Harvest Prayer Ministries
National Coordinator, National Prayer Committee
2785 Blue Ball Rd.
Rineyville, KY 40162
(812) 208-1836
jeff@harvestprayer.com

Areas of expertise: *Praying leadership, corporate prayer, Spirit-empowered ministry, prayer team training, leading concerts of prayer, developing your personal prayer life.*

Note: Jeff books all of Harvest's speakers. Go to www.harvestprayer.com for more information.

Olson, Dana

Director, Prayer First
2002 S. Arlington Heights Rd
Arlington Heights, IL 60005
(847) 879-3234
bigdana@aol.com

Areas of expertise: *Prayer First weekends include biblical call to prayer, various prayer subjects with biblical teaching and practical application, leading various prayer gatherings so people "taste and see" that it is GREAT!*
Preview audio tape available on request.

Poinsett, Brenda
Christian Communicator (author, teacher, speaker)
406 Edgewood Rd.
Union, MO 63084
(636) 584-0631
bpoinsett@yhti.net
Areas of expertise: *Prayer life of Jesus, prayer basics, conversational prayer, the Model Prayer (Lord's Prayer), creating life-changing small prayer groups.*
Preview audio tapes available on request.

Smith, Eddie and Alice
Eddie & Alice Smith Ministries
7710-T Cherry Park Dr., Ste 224
Houston, TX 77095
(800) 569-4825
Areas of expertise: *Intimate intercession, practical intercession, strategic prayer, spiritual warfare and mapping.*
Preview audio tape available on request to senior pastors.

VanderGriend, Dr. Alvin J.
Prayer Evangelism Associate, Harvest Prayer Ministries
606 Woodcreek Dr.
Lynden, WA 98264

(360) 354-5072
alvin@harvestprayer.com
Areas of expertise: *Personal and corporate prayer, developer of Learning to Love to Pray seminar and 40 Days of Prayer initiative.*
Preview video tape available on request.

Winger, Dr. Joseph
Pastor of Prayer, New Life Church
4215 Apple Hill Ct.
Colorado Springs, CO 80920
(719) 351-3296
jwinger@newlifechurch.org
Areas of expertise: *Mobilizing men to pray, spiritual warfare, praying for the lost, the Holy Spirit and prayer, prayer basics, city-wide prayer*

initiatives, prayer journeys.

Appendix B

Guidelines for Bringing in a Speaker

Travel

If flying, budget for $400-$450. Often a ticket can be purchased for less, but be prepared—especially if flying into a smaller-market airport. If you can afford to do so, offer to pay for the speaker's spouse to come as well. Most speakers travel so much this can be a nice gesture.

It is usually best to allow a speaker to purchase his or her own ticket. Give a dollar figure that you do not want to go over—if they cannot find a ticket within the budget by a certain time, a mutual decision to raise the amount can be made. Many churches have a travel agent—or a person who feels they know their way around the discount airline internet sites—and they prefer to book the ticket. The problem with this is that often mistakes are made, or in an effort to save $50, significant inconveniences are placed upon the speaker. I have had situations where I had to travel 90 minutes to leave from another airport (instead of 20 minutes to my usual airport) to save $100. It cost me more than four hours of extra time—(having a 90-minute drive home after getting in at midnight was not pleasant). Yes, you can get good deals on the internet; but they often come with very inconvenient times, long layovers, and three flights instead of two. You want your speaker to be relaxed and well rested when he or she arrives, not frazzled, hungry and grumpy due to an awful flight situation. Pay the extra $100 and get the best flights for your speaker.

Honorarium

Many speakers have a set fee for speaking. But many do not. They will often leave it up to the church. So what do you pay when that happens? How do you determine how much is fair? Generally you should consider both how many seminars/sermons your speaker has to deliver, and how many days he or she has to be away from his or her home. To provide $100 to $250 for a speaker who only speaks on Sunday, but has to fly in on Saturday and fly out on Monday is probably a little inadequate ($200 per day—including travel days—is probably a bare minimum to consider). Remember that this weekend may be the speaker's entire income (salary, plus social security, healthcare, office expenses, etc.) for a week or two. Most churches offer between $750 and $2,000 for a weekend. Some churches take a love offering, but again consider when you will take it. Will you take it on Sunday when a lot of people are present or at the seminar that 50 people come to? Will you take it by passing a plate or simply putting one in the back? You may need to be prepared to subsidize the offering if it is low. Also, a love offering should not be taken to cover the church's expenses, but should be given to the speaker.

Housing

Many churches save money by putting your guest in a private home. This is certainly acceptable, and many speakers enjoy this. But if it is within your church's ability to do so, ask the speaker which he or she would prefer. It is not that he or she does not like to socialize, but many prefer a hotel. Why? Often a speaker either gets very wound up or exhausted when speaking. Instead of feeling like he or she has to entertain the hosts—or be entertained—it is more relaxing to be alone in a hotel room. For me (Jon Graf) I prefer hotels because I like to work. I get high speed internet or hook up my computer to the phone line and work online. I often cannot do that in a person's house because there is no wireless internet or I tie up the only phone line. We also recommend putting a speaker up in a middle or upper value hotel. It costs more, but can make a lot of difference in the ability to relax. While less expensive hotels can be clean and comfortable, the biggest advantage of a higher quality hotel is the noise level between rooms (they are usually better insulated) and the ability to get food when hungry later at night. (And in most lower-value hotels the towels are like sandpaper!)

Meals

Most speakers prefer to eat with people—whether in homes or in restaurants. Having different members take the speaker out each meal is a wonderful idea to allow people to get to know him or her. One thing to keep in mind: prepare your people to not be offended if the speaker doesn't eat a lot, or doesn't take everything on the table. Those who travel a lot, end up eating too many big meals. They begin to get very particular as a matter of health. It is also a good idea to check with a speaker ahead of time to see if he or she has any dietary needs.

—Guidelines prepared by Jonathan Graf, president of the Church Prayer Leaders Network. Jonathan is a frequent speaker at church seminars and other prayer events. Used by permission.

Appendix c

Who I Am in Christ

Meditate on what Christ purchased for you on the cross. This is only a partial list of the way God feels about you.

I am more than a conqueror – *Rom. 8:37.*
I am the head and not the tail – *Deut. 28:13.*
I am created in His image – *Gen. 1:27.*
I was made just a little lower than God – *Ps. 8:5 (NAS, NLT).*
I am a spring of living water – *Jn. 7:38.*
I am an agent of change for good – *Mt. 5:13-14.*
I am my beloveds (and He is mine) – *SS. 2:16.*
I am fearfully and wonderfully made – *Ps. 139:13-14.*
I am known by God – *Gal. 4:9.*
I am accepted – *Eph. 1:6.*
I am God's child – *Rom. 8:16.*
I am a friend of Jesus Christ – *Jn. 15:15.*
I am His lover – *SS. 1:15.*

I have been justified – *Rom. 3:23-24.*
I am united with the Lord, I am one with Him and have been bought with an incredible price and I belong to God – *1 Cor. 6:19-20.*
I am a member of Christ's body – *Eph. 1:22-23.*
I was hand-picked by God and adopted as His child – *Rom. 8:15.*
I have been redeemed and forgiven of all my sins – *Col. 1:14.*
I am complete in Christ – *Col. 2:10.*
I have direct access to the throne of grace through Jesus Christ – *Heb. 4:16.*
I am free from condemnation – *Rom. 8:1.*
I am assured that God works for my good – *Rom. 8:28.*
I cannot be separated from the love of God – *Rom. 8:39.*
I have been established, anointed and sealed by God – *Col. 3:3.*
I am hidden with Christ in God – *Col. 3:3.*
I am confident that God will complete the good work He started in me – *Phil. 1:6.*
I am a citizen of Heaven – *Phil. 3:20.*
I have not been given a spirit of fear but of power, love and a sound mind – *2 Tim. 1:7.*
I am born of God – *1 Jn. 5:4.*
I am a branch of Jesus Christ, the true vine—a channel of His life – *Jn. 15:1.*
I am God's temple – *1 Cor. 6:19.*
I am seated with Jesus Christ in the heavenly realm – *Eph. 2:6.*
I am God's workmanship – *Eph. 2:10.*
I can do all things through Christ who strengthens me – *Phil. 4:13.*
I have the mind of Christ – *1 Cor. 2:16.*
I have access to the power that turned dead flesh into a resur-

rected, living, glorified, incorruptible body – *Eph. 1:19-20.*

I am His great delight – *Ps. 18:19.*

I am a partaker of His divine nature – *2 Pet. 1:4.*

I am set apart for Him – *Ps. 4:3.*

I am not under law but under grace – *Rom. 6:14.*

I am God's fellow-worker – *1 Cor. 3:9.*

I am God's field – *1 Cor. 3:9.*

I am God's building – *1 Cor. 3:9.*

I am competent to judge – *1 Cor. 6:2.*

I am a letter from Christ written by the
Spirit of the Living God – *2 Cor. 3:3.*

I am Abraham's seed—the fulfillment of
God's promise – *Gal. 3:29.*

I am blessed – *Gal. 3:9, Eph. 1:3.*

I am free – *Jn. 8:36.*

I am His pleasure – *Rev. 4:11.*

I am commissioned by God – *Mk. 16:15-18.*

I am captivating, beautiful – *Ps. 45:11.*

I am royalty – *1 Pet. 2:9; Rev. 5:10.*

Appendix D

Praying on Your Armor

Here is a sample prayer for praying on your armor. This is suggested only to give you an idea of how this might be done. As you pray through each piece, meditate on its benefits and uses, thanking God for making it available to us through Christ Jesus.

Father, today I choose to put on the Belt of Truth. I refuse to receive any of Satan's lies; I receive only Your truth. I break any words spoken over me that are not wholly and completely from You. I choose to deal truthfully with everyone I come in contact with today.

I take up the Breastplate of Righteousness. Father, I thank You that when You look at me You see the righteousness of Your Son, Jesus. I thank You not only for Your forgiveness of the sins I have committed, but also for the victory

won for me on the Cross to live no longer as a slave to sin but as a slave to righteousness. I receive that victory and choose to walk in it today.

I put on my Shoes of Peace. I choose to be anxious for nothing, giving thanks in everything. I choose to live acknowledging that You are in control. I choose to live in Your gospel of love which casts out all fear.

I take up my Shield of Faith—thank You that it blocks every fiery dart of the enemy. I thank You that if You do allow a dart to penetrate that shield, it is transformed into refining fire for a purpose. I receive that refining fire from You for Your Glory. I choose to walk in faith today. I ask You to multiply my faith—I know it is not possible to please You without faith. I eagerly desire the gift of bold, radical faith.

Father, I pray on my Helmet of Deliverance. I refuse every thought from the enemy and take captive every thought in the Name of the Lord Jesus Christ of Nazareth Who came in the flesh. I ask for wisdom today and choose to walk in that without double-mindedness. I choose today to have the mind of Christ over every situation.

Thank You, Father for the Sword of the Spirit. I appropriate that piece of the armor today. I stand on Your Word and Your Word alone. Light my path with it, Lord. Teach me Your ways; guide me in the way of all Truth for Your Word is Truth.

Above all, I take up my weapon of prayer. I pray for my enemies; I bless them, Lord. I pray for those in authority and for those who struggle with living out their faith. Father, I pray for _______ who struggles as I have with the sin of ______________________. Help them stand firm in Jesus Name. Holy Spirit, remind me continuously to appropriate prayer and thankfulness throughout this day as I pray for all the saints.